PALM TREES ON THE HUDSON

A True Story of the Mob,
Judy Garland & Interior Decorating

Elliot Tiber

SQUAREONE
PUBLISHERS

You may be wondering why a nonfiction work would have a disclaimer. Well, it boils down to a nervous publisher who worries about using real names when describing a crooked judge, a connected restaurateur, and their cronies. So for the sake of his sanity, I changed almost everyone's name except for those of my idol, Judy Garland; Mayor Lindsay, who was never a crook; and my family members. If any names resemble those of people living or dead—or if any place names resemble those of real places, past or present—please be aware that this is merely a coincidence. Of course, for those curious readers who want to know the real names of bad guys, there's always Google.

Concerning all that took place between me and the divine Miss Garland, every piece of it is absolutely true. And in the face of any yellow-brick-road journalists who may come around, let me hereby warn you that I own a pair of red ruby slippers and I'm not afraid to wear them! As for the man from whom I rented all those palm trees, if you're still out there, sir, I hope this book will finally explain what the hell happened to them.

IN-HOUSE EDITOR: Joanne Abrams
TYPESETTER: Gary A. Rosenberg
COVER DESIGN: Jeannie Tudor
COVER ART: Bobby Hill
www.resetuniverse.com
BACK COVER PHOTO: Payam Rahimian
www.payam.com

Square One Publishers
115 Herricks Road
Garden City Park, NY 11040
(516) 535-2010 • (877) 900-BOOK
www.SquareOnePublishers.com

Library of Congress Cataloging-in-Publication Data

Tiber, Elliot, 1935-
  Palm trees on the Hudson : a true story of the mob, Judy Garland, & interior decorating / Elliot Tiber.
    p. cm.
  ISBN 978-0-7570-0351-6 (hardcover)
  1. Tiber, Elliot, 1935- 2. Gay men—New York (State)—Biography. 3. Interior decorators—New York (State) I. Title.
  HQ75.8.T53T527 2011
  306.76'62092—dc22
  [B]

Printed in the United States of America

10   9   8   7   6   5   4   3   2   1

Contents

This book is dedicated to Andre Ernotte,
my long-term companion and cherished friend,
whom I trust is out there somewhere,
still sharing my joie de vivre and remembrances of things past.

Acknowledgments

First, I give my heartfelt thanks to my sister Renee for her tenderness and encouragement. Her sharp humor helped me in the writing of this book and made the Hudson River Walkway all the more enjoyable.

I also thank my cherished friends Alyce Finell, Joan Wilen, Lydia Wilen, and Scott Hall, for guiding my literary talents away from mayhem, madness, and complete "outré."

Thanks to all of you who have been supportive of me in the past, present, and future:

Judy Garland
Molly Picon
Calvin Ki
Joseph and Gail Papp
Zubin Mehta
Neal Burstein, Esq.
Andy Roth of The Agency
  Group
Lybi Ma
Jack Blumkin, CPA
Marti Mabin and David
  Schnitter
Nancy and Roger Cunningham

Claude Lombard
Annie Cordy
Bernard Giraudeau
Anny Duperey
Roy Howard and Jeryl
  Abramson
Larry Dvoskin
Dr. Rod Hurt
Stan Goldstein
Dr. Michael Weiner
Katharine Hepburn
Bette Davis
Michael Moriarty

André Bishop of Lincoln
  Center Theater
Marlon Brando
Tennessee Williams
Truman Capote
Ingrid Bergman
RTB TV Brussels
National Theater of Belgium
Linda Lepomme
Editions Rossel of Belgium
President Giscard D'Estaing
Queen Fabiola
Golda Meir
Life Magazine
Richie Havens
Janis Joplin
Jimi Hendrix
Sammy Davis, Jr.
Arlo Guthrie
Pete Seeger
Federico Fellini
Pier Pasolini
Harvey Milk

Jade Marx and Dom Ruiz
Congressman Barney Frank
Yuri and Rita Brisker
Alyse, Steve, and Scott
  Peterson
Beverly Dates
Rachelle Teichberg Golden and
  Sam Golden
Roger Orcutt
Fanny Ernotte
Marcia Lewison
Irving and Lee Regent
Suzy Falk
Charles Murray
Paul Adler
Robert Mapplethorpe
Marion Florsheim
Walter Bahno
Shirley Kaplan
Robin and Steve Kaufman
Max Yasgur
The Manhattan Plaza family
Jack Teichberg

A special thanks to Ang Lee, James Schamus, and the Focus Features family.

I am grateful to my publisher, Rudy Shur of Square One, and to Square One's Anthony Pomes and Joanne Abrams. I am especially thankful to Rich Mintzer, without whom this book would have been a single 240-page sentence.

Finally, I thank my ever-loving Yorkies, Molly Picon, Shayna, and Woody Woodstock.

1

Judy and the Free Dish

The movie house went dark, and I found myself watching a girl who seemed not much older than I was. Within minutes, her tiny dog was taken away from her, a storm separated her from her family, and her weathered farmhouse was ripped from the earth and spun around like a top. The events in this girl's stark black-and-white world were happening so quickly and were so alarming that I felt tearful and afraid. But then, suddenly and unexpectedly, the screen lit up in dazzling Technicolor, soft music played in the background, and the girl's world became one of enchantment. Dorothy Gale was in a beautiful sunlit land far away from her home in Kansas—and far away from mine in Bensonhurst, Brooklyn, too. She was in the Land of Oz.

Dorothy sang and danced her way through her magical new world, caught between a desire for adventure and a hunger for her safe and loving home. I was totally absorbed in the movie, hypnotized by the story and all the strange and exotic characters. No one in this film looked like the people who trudged down the crowded, dreary streets of Brooklyn. Instead, Dorothy—clad in a gingham dress and gleaming ruby slippers—skipped down a shining yellow brick road accompanied by her faithful dog, Toto; a talking scarecrow; a lovable tin man; and a cowardly lion. I wanted so much to follow her, to be one of her new friends, to share in her journey.

The Wizard of Oz captivated me as no film had before. Like every child, I was entranced by the songs, the colorful costumes, and Dorothy's thrilling adventures. But the movie also spoke to me in a very personal way. When Dorothy sang "Over the Rainbow," I was spellbound not only by her beautiful voice, but also by the longing and hope she expressed. Like me, Dorothy felt out of step with her everyday world and dreamed of a trouble-free home where she would be loved, accepted, and happy. Could it be that the longed-for world actually existed for me as well, far away from my real-life existence of screaming parents and family arguments?

To say that the movie had a profound effect on me would be an understatement. For the first time in my eight years of life, I felt a connection to another person. Maybe it was a childish crush, or perhaps it was simply the fact that this girl dreamed of a better place and actually found it. Whatever it was, the few hours I spent in the theater couldn't have been a more enjoyable experience— except for the woman sitting next to me, nudging me with her elbow throughout the movie, saying "Elli, stop shuckling around in your seat, you're gonna drop the plate." The woman was my mother. For me, Elliot Teichberg, going to the movies every week was an escape from the lunacy I called home. For Momma, however, it was all business.

With the war raging in Europe, movie theaters were hard-pressed to pull in paying customers during the week. In an effort to attract more patrons, especially women, they began to offer a free dish on certain evenings. When the old Metro theater, a rundown former vaudeville playhouse, began its Plate Night promotion every Tuesday, the giveaway was not lost on my mother. Each week, a different dish was handed out. Sometimes it was a soup bowl; other times, a dinner plate. Every once in a while, the hard-to-come-by gravy boat was offered. Hundreds of different pieces were given away, one piece at a time, enabling frequent moviegoers to acquire a massive set of dishes.

For Momma, this was an opportunity to cash in. She didn't care very much about what was playing at the theater. For her, it was a simple business transaction. On Tuesday nights, she took me to the Metro, and on Thursdays, she took my youngest sister Renee to another local theater that had its own Plate Night. Children under ten got in for free, so for the price of just one ticket, mother got two dishes. What did she do with them? That was the beauty of it. She arranged them in the front window of her housewares store, where she would sell them to women who were hoping to complete their own partial sets or to those ladies who didn't know you could get the dishes for the price of a movie ticket.

For me, it was a perfect arrangement. Momma got what she wanted, and I enjoyed a temporary escape—a place where I could lose myself for a couple of hours. Of course, I quickly learned how to hold onto a dish without dropping it, but that was a small price to pay. I wasn't about to give up my Tuesdays at the movies because of a broken plate.

I knew that Momma couldn't care less about what I was feeling. As soon as a movie ended, she would pull me out of my seat, abruptly breaking the spell cast by the story. But tonight, not even Momma could drag me out of Oz. The sights and sounds of this movie filled my head. Sure, I had a box of magic tricks at home and a magic wand that I had made from a twig I found in our garden. But not even with the sparkling glitter I'd glued on did it compare to the magic I saw in the movie. My box of tricks didn't sing and dance; it didn't transport me to an enchanted world. After seeing *The Wizard of Oz,* I could never enjoy that box of nothing again.

In 1943, I knew practically nothing about Judy Garland other than how she moved me as the character of Dorothy, but I was instantly smitten and hopelessly hooked. I knew I would always have a special place in my heart for her. What I couldn't have predicted was how she would become an icon for the gay community, which had yet to loudly and proudly announce itself to the world. Nor could I have guessed the impact she would have on my own life as a gay man and artist. But we'll get to that later. For now, let me start my story by introducing the Teichbergs of Brooklyn—a family not so much over the rainbow as over the cuckoo's nest.

2

Meet the
Teichbergs

My parents were among the millions of Jewish immigrants who
fled Eastern Europe in hopes of a better life in America. Momma
and her large family of fifteen brothers and sisters managed to
escape extermination by precious seconds as Cossack soldiers
burned their tiny village in Russia. They stuffed potatoes in their
pockets and fled through the heavy snowdrifts by foot, finally
reaching the seaport. Sadly, only Momma and three of her brothers
could find room on the ship that transported them away from their
homeland. The rest of the family would perish in the cholera epi-
demic of 1910.

Pop and his family of eight left Austria right before the beginning of World War One and also headed to America, land of
dreams. They would settle in the Borough Park section of Brooklyn,
a largely Jewish community of immigrants who spoke Russian, Ger-

man, and Yiddish—often at the same time. My dad's father, Yunnel, was a roofer, and that skill came in handy whenever the old thatched roofs in the neighborhood needed work. The Teichbergs had brought some money from their homeland and purchased a three-story brownstone from which Grandpa Yunnel could run his roofing business on the ground floor, while the family made its home on the two upper floors.

My dad, the oldest of six children, worked alongside his father and learned the roofing business. The money that he and his father made went to send his sisters and brothers to college. They all became professionals—two lawyers, a dentist, an architect, and a pharmacist. My father's siblings looked down on him because he was a laborer. As a result, he almost never spoke to any of them.

My parents met in Brooklyn at a social function held by a local community group. Since there were so many Jewish immigrants in Borough Park and the surrounding neighborhoods, social events were held so that everyone could meet, socialize, and speak Yiddish—all in an attempt to marry off their children. Such was the case with my parents. Old photos showed that Momma was once stunning, bearing an uncanny resemblance to the 1920s "It" Girl, Clara Bow. Pop, to my eyes, was as handsome as Errol Flynn. They were married in 1919, despite my father's parents' strong and repeated objections to their son's choice of a mate. Looking back now at the matrimonial example my parents set, I find myself ever more in favor of arranged marriages.

Dad's proven trade skill, developed at a young age, was beneficial since he was able to start his own roofing business immediately after the wedding. Momma, meanwhile, worked as a seamstress in the garment district of lower Manhattan. At home, she quickly assumed the role of money manager for the family based upon two simple economic principles: Spend as little as possible, and if you ever have to spend, always pay below cost. Fortunately for my parents, they were able to keep working even as the Great Depression took its toll on most Americans. As a result, Momma saved up about three thousand dollars—a good deal of money in those days, and enough to buy a large private house in Bensonhurst, where I was born. The previous owner had apparently committed suicide somewhere in the house, so when the bank foreclosed on the property, there were few potential buyers interested in a "bad luck" house. With or without luck, Momma purchased the place at a third of its value.

It would be easy to call the Teichberg house a "nondescript" stucco one-family structure. However, it was descript—it was really ugly. The house had a main floor with a living room, dining room, kitchen, and bathroom. Upstairs were three bedrooms, and above that, an attic. There was no sense of style inside or out. But whatever the interior lacked in design was obscured by the mishmash of furnishings. Rhyme, reason, color, and fashion had no bearing on Momma's arrangement of furniture. If it was free—or, at least, didn't cost very much—and if my father could fix it, it soon found a place in the house. If I had to come up with a style, I would say "Early Salvation Army Rejects."

The house came with a large finished basement, which Momma rented out to a lovely black couple. The man worked as a bookkeeper, while the woman cleaned homes. They were kind, friendly, well-dressed, and knew how to fix up an apartment. In other words, they had all the qualities my parents seemed to lack. While my parents were always cordial to them, during the ten years they spent living in our home, I overheard Momma telling my dad that she was worried they might steal from us. "Steal what?" I thought. There was nothing in that house that anyone would want to take!

🌴 🌴 🌴

It was in the giant stucco house that my parents started their family. First came my sister Goldie. Four years later, my sister Rachelle arrived. I was born nine years later; and two years after that, my baby sister Renee joined the party. Yes, there were now six of us living in the middle of Brooklyn, a borough best known at the time for Coney Island, Nathan's hot dogs, and the Brooklyn Dodgers. Our neighborhood, Bensonhurst, was made up of a crowded mass of brick-and-stone buildings and houses that formed a city within a city. Unlike the more elegant avenues that lined Manhattan, there was a hodgepodge of two-story buildings, each of which had a store on the ground floor and dreary apartments on the second level. An expansive mix of private houses were also strewn about every which way, wherever the rows of stores ended. Immigrant Jewish families that had settled in New York made up most of the local population. Many of these families had earned enough money to escape the poverty of Manhattan's Lower East Side, where most of the immigrants had gathered in the early years of the twentieth century.

In the middle of this busy enclave, Momma found an investment opportunity. On the corner of Seventieth Street and Twentieth Avenue, there sat a two-story house with two rental apartments and a storefront. The price was right. The rentals would pay for the upkeep of the building, and Momma could then start a business. The store was located on a corner with display windows on either side. It sat catty-cornered between a grocery store and a candy store, and was a short walk from our house. My dad built shelves along the walls, and near the front door was Momma's Holy Grail—the cash register. It was ancient, but it held the money. The store would be Momma's own hardware and housewares store where she would sell anything even remotely related to the home.

So when I was born, this store was apparently to be my birthright, or at least my home away from home. When I was little, Momma would drag me there and leave me to my own devices. So with fanciful abandon, I would rummage through the merchandise. In the basement of the store were floor-to-ceiling boxes filled with all sorts of things—pots, pans, dishes, paints, and all manner of knickknacks. It provided a lot of possibilities for a young child. In the store, I liked to throw down can openers, pots, screwdrivers, potholders, and especially light bulbs. The bulbs would make this loud *pop!* sound as they hit the store floor, and this sound resonated with me enormously. Momma and Pop, on the other hand, were not pleased. To Momma, those breaking bulbs sounded like precious coins being flushed down a toilet, and to Pop, they were a prelude to Momma's braying scream. This would be followed by the *thwack!* of his trouser belt slapping my toddler bottom.

Sometimes, when the store was busy, Momma dumped me onto a keg of nails as she rushed to make a sale. I turned that into another game that I enjoyed immensely. Basically, I would toss fistfuls of hardware across the floor until some busybody customer hustled over and told me, "Do not throw the nails on the floor, little boy!" The well-meaning buttinsky would then inform Momma that her cute little boy was throwing nails all over the floor. Momma's response? "Lady? You want to buy nails? If you ain't buying nails, get away from my son!" Suffice it to say that she did not possess good customer relation skills.

As I got older, I progressed from playing in the store to working there. Even before I was tall enough to reach the cash register, Momma felt that I should busy myself by putting nails in a bag or placing merchandise on some of the lower shelves. While this provided more of a purpose to my activities, it did not provide me with any reward because Momma didn't pay me for my labor—not even an allowance. Although business was brisk, Momma's desire to make money (and keep it) far outweighed any wish to make her son feel appreciated. She was the epitome of frugality and practicality, and to her, it was not practical to pay her son when he would work for nothing!

Momma's store was run seemingly without rules and without any discernible sense of organization. No items were marked with prices. Whenever a customer showed an interest in something, Momma dreamed up a price on the spot. When my father and I unpacked stock, we just shoved it onto the shelves. Sometimes Pop simply cut off the box top and placed the carton outside on the sidewalk. Strangely, few things were ever stolen. Perhaps the neighborhood criminals were scared of Momma. I know I was.

Hanging around the store didn't bother me, since I was not inclined to spend much time playing with the other kids. Unathletic and socially awkward, I had few friends, and filled most of my hours by spinning about in Momma's store or, on weekends, helping Pop with the roofing business. Growing up, I just assumed every kid had an after-school job that spilled over into the weekend.

Momma managed to squirrel away the money from her store, from Poppa's roofing business, and from their property rentals. Any gifts we received, any household items that neighbors left on the sidewalk, and anything that the rest of us found on the street immediately became salable merchandise for her shop. Momma was ready to sell almost anything, and I sometimes feared that our dog, Sandy, would literally become the doggie in the window. Sure, Momma had her tender and understanding side. For instance, she would let me keep any string I found around the store so I could make a ball from my findings. More often than not, though, Momma claimed we had no money for such luxuries as comic books, games, chewing gum, birthday presents—even new clothes. She had no problem asking neighbors and relatives if they had hand-me-down clothes for her children to wear. We led a meager lifestyle, but somewhere, Momma had piles of cash. And of course, I had a sixty-pound ball of string!

🌴　🌴　🌴

At a very early age, I was keenly aware that Momma and Pop were not well-suited to parenthood. Between the roofing business and working at the store, my dad labored sixteen hours a day, and knowing Momma, he probably wasn't getting paid either. Pop's one and only recreational activity was fighting with Momma, almost always over money and never about raising me or my sisters. He would start out very slowly and quietly, almost always deferring to Momma's shouted commands. He wouldn't speak until it got to be too much for him, and then the fireworks would begin. When my parents fought at the store, the battle took precedence over any customers who happened to be present. In fact, shoppers appeared to relish the Teichberg sideshow. I, on the other hand, was so upset by all the screaming that I would run and hide in the basement. I was too young to realize that if I had sold tickets to my parents' fights, I would have finally made some money off of my mother's store.

Dad and I shared very few father-and-son moments. In one failed attempt at an outing, he took me to see a Brooklyn Dodgers game. One of Pop's roofing customers had given him two free tickets so that Mr. Teichberg and his only son could enjoy a day at the ball park. Since I had no idea who the players were on either team or what the rules might be, my only real interest was in the hot dogs and peanuts. As for the game, it bored both of us to death; Pop was no more a sports fan than I was. Looking back, all I can say is that we both tried hard to connect and failed miserably.

The one thing that did give my father pleasure in his routine existence was his Cadillac. Dad had bought a used Cadillac before I was born, sometime during the Great Depression. It was his pride and joy. Since my parents never spent money on anything but essentials, they had cash when nobody else did. We weren't exactly rich, but riding around in this huge car made people think we were. Later in life, I realized that the car was also his way of saying, "I am not whipped by my wife. She let me buy this car." If that had really been true, my father might have enjoyed his life a little bit more.

While my father had little time or inclination for proper parenting, now and then, he was able to muster up the energy needed to give me a good thrashing at Momma's fanatical command. I knew that he took out his aggression towards Momma on me—and I think he knew that I knew. Whether I had stocked the shelves at the store incorrectly, failed to straighten up my room, fought with one of my sisters, or committed one of a dozen other minor infractions, he was always able to summon the strength to wallop me—and I always had enough buried empathy to understand.

Although Momma never hit me, her attacks were psychological and therefore even worse than my heated sessions with Pop. Both in word and deed, Momma frequently told me that I was worthless.

Having made myself overweight by stuffing myself with chocolate bars and soda, I already felt fat and ugly. Momma provided that little something extra needed to destroy any chance I had of developing self-esteem. Momma was, however, very loving to my sisters. Being girls, they were all expected to find good Jewish husbands, get married, and have babies. As the only son, more was expected of me. What that "more" was, though, I had no idea.

🌴　🌴　🌴

Despite the fact that I was expected to spend hours working in Momma's store and weekends assisting Pop in the roofing business, I did manage to occasionally escape from my parents and enjoy an hour or two on my own. Because so much of my childhood was spent working, though, I wasn't always sure what I wanted to do with my free time.

On a handful of occasions, I visited the boy who had just moved in next door. Dominick came from a large Italian family. His father, uncles, and other relatives seemed to come and go at all hours, day and night, but he was usually at home. A year younger than I was, Dominick was certainly much stronger and liked to demonstrate that fact by hitting and punching me. For some odd reason, I did not seem to mind it very much. The physical contact, rough though it was, did not upset me the way my father's whippings did. Dominick also loved to wave toy guns around, and there seemed to be plenty of them in his house. Dominick's family was very different from mine. They intimidated me and made me uncomfortable, so I didn't spend that much time with him.

For the most part, I spent my "time off" with my sister Renee, who was two years my junior. The two of us played all sorts of games such as Monopoly, Go Fish, Casino, and Parcheesi. Renee really didn't understand the games, so I made up simple rules that she could comprehend as we played. At other times, we would go outdoors and jump rope or play hide and seek. Occasionally, we would go roller skating. Mom sold roller skates in the store, so that was the one piece of "sports equipment" we had.

When Renee and I got bored, we would sometimes snoop around the house, checking out closets in our parents' room or in other parts of the house. It was on one of these investigative missions that I discovered an Underwood typewriter. I didn't remember ever seeing anyone use it and I was surprised that it hadn't been sold in the store, like everything else we had of any value.

I started to peck away at the keyboard, and in time, I managed to learn how to type. I just loved tapping away at the letters and seeing printed words appear on the paper, which I had also found buried deep in a closet. At first, I wrote silly stories—whatever came to mind. I would read them out loud to Renee, and she would laugh at what she understood. Although I didn't realize it at the time, my little sister looked up to me and always wanted to take part in whatever I was doing. Had I been aware of Renee's hero worship, I would have told her that I was not to be considered a role model. But neither one of us was getting any real attention from Momma and Pop, so for a time, we filled up the emptiness of our home with each other's company.

While it was fun to share my writings with Renee, when I was about ten years old, I decided to turn my hobby into a business. Perhaps it was in my blood to try to earn money; after all, it was all I had ever learned from my parents. My idea was to use my newfound typing skills to edit and publish a one-page newspaper called *The 73rd Street Gazette,* named for the street on which we lived.

In most movie Westerns, I had seen yellowed newspapers that always seemed to be called *The Gazette*. I figured out how to type three vertical columns and headlines, and used carbon paper to produce several dozen copies of each week's edition. Despite its official-sounding name, *The Gazette* offered non sequitur observations of the games being played by neighborhood kids, the rantings of their mothers, and, of course, stories of the old men who wheeled wagons from which they sold hot potatoes in the winter and colored water with sweet flavoring in the summer. I also wrote about the assortment of men who wandered down the street yelling, "I cash clothes!" Stay-at-home wives and mothers would rush down from their apartments to sell a blouse, a coat, or a pair of pants. I never understood what the vendors did with the used clothing and why they paid cash for it. Like any cub reporter, I constantly put my nose in everyone else's business. For some reason, though, I couldn't pluck up the courage to question the cash-for-clothes crew.

Renee and I would stand in busy neighborhood areas and sell our papers for two cents each. My *73rd Street Gazette* was a success for several months; then disaster struck. It all started with Phyllis Tudanger, one of my sister Rachelle's girlfriends, whose breasts were, shall we say, more than amply proportioned. In the wartime jargon of the age, she was sporting some mighty sizeable torpedoes on her upper deck. The Tudanger Boobs were a popular subject of neighborhood discussion, not only with the boys but also with the girls. All the kids, including me, had a basic curiosity about human anatomy and found it most entertaining to watch the Boobs bop up and down under Phyllis's angora sweaters as she walked around town. Naturally, I decided to write about this phenomenon in my weekly paper. All well and good until Phyllis's mother got her hands on a copy and went storming over to my parents' house. Mrs. Tudanger ranted and raved in Yiddish about the terrible embarrassment and shame that I had caused her family. I couldn't understand why she and my parents were carrying on about something that everyone was already talking about. Nevertheless, Pop locked away the typewriter, putting *The Gazette* out of business. Had I known that this kind of censorship existed, I might have thought twice about running the story—or at least made up a fictitious name for Phyllis.

The grass did not have time to grow under my feet before I threw myself into an entirely new enterprise. Our house came with two garages. Since the Cadillac was our only car, Momma decided to make a little extra money by renting out the other garage to the driver of a 7UP truck. This was good for me, because I now had a full inventory of 7UP bottles at my disposal. Since my drink of choice was Pepsi, I started selling the 7UP at two cents a bottle. It was a great success for a couple of weeks because the neighborhood candy stores sold the very same soda for eight cents a bottle. When the driver of the truck discovered that his merchandise was disappearing, though, he complained to my father. I didn't know that I was doing anything wrong, so I made no attempt to deny that I had established a very successful soda-pop business. Had he carried Pepsi, I told the driver, I would have taken the bottles for myself. Apparently, Pop was not impressed with my honesty. To make the point, he gave me a spanking—this time, without any prodding from Momma. He then put a new lock on the garage door, and I was again out of business.

🌴 🌴 🌴

When I turned twelve, I began suffering through Hebrew lessons in preparation for my bar mitzvah. While a bar mitzvah is standard practice for any Jewish boy, Momma also had the firm yet mis-guided belief that I was going to attend the yeshiva high school and then go on to become a rabbi. I had seen rabbis on the Jewish hol-idays when we would go to synagogue. The thought of being the one who stood up in front of everyone at temple and read through mountains of Hebrew in supplication to the Lord was not exactly my big dream. At twelve years of age, I still had no idea what I wanted to be when I grew up. All I really knew was that I did not want to be a rabbi. No Talmudic scholar was I. A lion, a tin man, or a scarecrow, maybe, but a rabbi, no.

There was, however, an advantage to studying Hebrew—it gave me a great reason to excuse myself from working in the store: "Sorry, can't work today, Momma. I've got to study Hebrew." Yes, this was my very own get-out-of-jail-free card. While I rarely played it, when I did, Momma accepted it without a squabble. This not only removed me from her all-seeing eyes, but also gave me more opportunity to explore entrepreneurial pursuits.

But this time, I realized that I had a certain amount of artistic talent, and it didn't take long to dream up a way that would harness my abilities into a business. Our local stationery store sold greeting cards for twenty-five cents each—sometimes fifty cents. I took eight-by-ten-inch sheets of paper and my watercolors, and began to design tree-, fruit-, and flower-decorated greeting cards. When I priced my handmade cards at only five cents apiece, they were an immediate hit. In fact, I couldn't make them fast enough. Of course, I didn't have a degree from the Harvard School of Business and didn't know that I should factor in my hours—nor did I know anything about a profit margin.

Renee, ever proud of my cleverness and eager to help, assisted me in distributing my cards. Together, we loaded them into a dented Red Flyer wagon—"on loan" from Momma's shop—and brought our wares directly to our neighbors. But this business, too, came to an abrupt end. Tired of schlepping the Red Flyer around town, I parked it in front of the stationery store, reasoning that this would be a logical place for the wagon since everyone who wanted a card would go to the shop, where they would conveniently find a cheaper alternative. Predictably, many shoppers bought my cards instead of going into the store. Then Mrs. Fifenagel, who owned the shop, waddled out to see why a crowd had assembled under her store awning. One look at me and my cards, and she let out a shriek of indignation. Then she practically pulled me up the block towards Teichberg's Housewares Store.

Momma did her best to make me understand that I had been stealing bread from Mrs. Fifenagel's mouth. I was confused, as I felt that I had done no such thing. Also, judging from Mrs. Fifenagel's size, the lady didn't have a problem getting bread or anything else into her mouth. Nevertheless, Momma promptly emptied out the red wagon and assured the shopkeeper that I would never again sell cards in front of her establishment. It was all way above me. I felt bad that my venture caused such a ruckus, and even worse when Momma sold my cards in her store and didn't give me a red cent in return. Adding insult to injury, she placed the dented red wagon back in the store window and sold it within a week. Once again, I was out of business—kaput. And though I still didn't know a lick of Hebrew, through my unfortunate business experiences, I was beginning to learn the meanings of Yiddish words such as "yutz," "putz," "schmendrick," "nudnick," and that immortal favorite, "schmuck."

🌴 🌴 🌴

As I entered my teens, my interest in art grew, and the fact that I had few art supplies became an increasing source of frustration. Without an allowance, I had no choice but to beg Momma for some oil paints and brushes, and perhaps a canvas or two. In her eyes, this was total madness, which she made crystal clear in her one-word response: "What?!" She then reminded me at great length that she had a mortgage to pay and food to put on the table—not that very much of the food ever left the table since Momma was such a frighteningly bad cook. Acting like a character in some insane Russian opera, Momma screeched that she had sacrificed everything for her family, and now here I was, asking her to throw out good money on *bupkis* (nothing).

With my bar mitzvah in the past, I was again working long hours in the store and on roofing jobs with Pop. I therefore—not unreasonably, I thought—requested that Momma pay me a salary. As always, she was quick to tell me how she had fled Mother Russia in the dead of winter with nothing but raw potatoes in her pockets. She told me how before I was born, she had worked in all the very worst New York sweatshops—ten hours a day, six days a week—and had saved every penny so that the proud Teichbergs could have enough money for a lovely house. As she said this, I thought, *Well, Momma, that lovely house must have not been available because we ended up living here!* But I was not so stupid that I would say that out loud. Instead, I dropped the matter and, later in the week, simply stole some house paint from her store and swiped some brushes from school.

One spring day, after a healthy lunch of potato chips, Pepsi, and Baby Ruth candy bars, I found myself staring at the blank walls of the Teichberg dining room. With no canvas available, those walls sure looked inviting. Momma was at work, as was Pop, so I had some time to myself. I moved the faux French provincial Salvation Army china cabinet from the wall, and then shoved the faux Jacobean sideboard out of the way. With excitement, I began to size up the expanse of blank walls.

Something in those empty walls spoke to me. This was better than any art store canvas, for sure. I opened up a few gallons of paint and impulsively painted a Brazilian rainforest tableau and bits of Disney jungle images. For good measure, and to achieve harmony and balance, I painted a yellow brick road winding its way through the middle of the jungle, and added a flying monkey or two skimming their way through the deep green foliage. Every time I added a new element, I felt stronger and more self-assured. Upon applying a final brush stroke, I stood back and drank in my work. *This house is finally a home,* I thought. Then I realized that one wall was simply not enough for my jungle, so I moved on to the other walls of the room.

It was just turning dark as I finally finished my masterpiece. Although exhausted, I felt happy and strangely at peace. But my serenity ended abruptly as Momma returned from the store and pierced the silence with her bird-like shrieks.

"Gottenu! What have you done, Eliyahu? Look at that schmutz on my nice clean dining room walls!" Of course, our house was never clean. Everything was always piled up with assorted furnishings, clothes, and chachkas, but I didn't think that this sage observation would make Momma any happier.

"Wait till your father gets home. You are going to get it! And now you will get no allowance! No movies, no toys, no vacations, no presents!" She seemed oblivious to the fact that we were never given any of these things anyway—except movies. While most of the threats meant little to me, Momma's capricious ban on films did upset me because I needed that steady supply of Tinseltown stars—Carmen Miranda, Betty Grable, and, of course, Judy Garland—to avoid losing my mind.

Momma made it clear that by the end of that weekend, the walls would be returned to white. As it turned out, though, fate had different plans. That Sunday afternoon, while Pop was busy mixing the paint that would obliterate my work of art, Momma was preparing her monthly charity card game for some neighbors. When the ladies arrived and walked through the dining room carrying platters of snacks, they were overwhelmed by the colorful jungle scenes that surrounded them. Speaking louder than even Momma, who was hastening to apologize for the ugly walls, one of the ladies exclaimed, "Oh, my God, Sonia. How absolutely beautiful! Look at the palm trees and the birdies. And that waterfall! Sooo beautiful!"

"Such class, Sonia. It must have cost a fortune!" Mrs. Yallowitz exclaimed.

As my mother's friends oohed and aahed, I beamed with joy. Momma, on the other hand, looked totally confused. She glanced at the ladies' upturned faces and then at mine. Suddenly, her confusion transformed into what could have passed for pride, if I hadn't known better.

Momma walked over to me, put her arm around my shoulders, and gave me a squeeze. "My son, Elli, he painted the jungle all by himself!" she said with unaccustomed delight. I never saw her show any pride in anything I did, nor anything that anyone else did, for that matter. When Pop stomped in carrying a can of white paint, she quickly shooed him out of the room. How could he even think of ruining such a work of art? His look of utter bewilderment enhanced the moment for me that much more.

"Elli, darling, how much would you charge to paint a mural in my dining room?" Mrs. Fishbein asked. I was thrilled. Artistic recognition is so hard to come by. That is a well-documented fact. Didn't Van Gogh have to cut off his ear before he achieved notice? I, however, had been given entrée to the walls of many other Bensonhurst homes. In the next few months, I painted a dozen dining rooms at a whopping twenty-five dollars each. I was making a living, of sorts, as an artist.

"I'll hold the money," Momma volunteered before I left for my first job at Mrs. Fishbein's house. "You'll waste it on comic books or someone will steal it from you," she insisted, with feigned concern for her offspring.

But it didn't matter. I had delighted other people with my own vision, my own creation. I knew now, for the first time, that Momma did not have to like or approve of what I did. I was not the failure she made me out to be. I had done something to spite her, and along the way, I had impressed her very own friends and even made a name for myself in the neighborhood. Of course, after her friends had left the house, Momma shook her head in disapproval. She did not see what the other ladies had seen. To her, I had defaced the beautiful, clean walls of her home. Certainly, she did not consider the fact that I might have talent. But she said nothing more about it because if people were willing to pay money for what I did, that was all that mattered.

I will never understand why I continued to seek my mother's approval in the years to come. But that day in our dining room, I not only succeeded as an entrepreneur, but also officially launched my career as an artist—even if Momma had no clue and Pop was taking a nap.

3

We're Not in Bensonhurst Anymore!

"I'll rent out your room! I'll change the locks! Don't come crying to me when you can't make it out there on your own with all those goyim! Then everyone will know how useless you are—how you are nothing without your Momma! Good riddance!"

These were Momma's supportive words when I finally got sick of living under her penny-pinching regime and decided to move out of the stucco house of horrors. I was eighteen years of age, had already completed several years of college, and could no longer stand the fighting, the frugality, or the relentless insults that characterized my life in the Teichberg household.

🌴 🌴 🌴

Momma had started me off in school a year earlier than all the other kids because she simply wanted to get me off her hands and focus on her business. As a result, I was only sixteen when I graduated from Midwood High School after completing my "sentence" at the yeshiva elementary school. Neither institution left a positive impression. I had few friends, few outside interests other than my art, and few fond memories of my pre-college years. I hoped that college would provide me with the freedom to take courses that actually interested me.

Since Brooklyn College was in Flatbush, a short trip from Bensonhurst, and my older sister Goldie had graduated from there with a degree in art, I applied for the fall freshman class. It wasn't my first choice, though. I had wanted to go to Pratt Art Institute and had saved the five hundred dollars from my bar mitzvah for that very purpose. Having endured the anguish of Hebrew lessons, attending Pratt would be my big reward. Of course, that plan died when Momma decided that she needed the money to fund Goldie's upcoming marriage. Goldie needed a lavish engagement party, a wedding dress, and a sectional sofa, and the only money that would pay for Goldie's needs was the cash I had earmarked for my education.

"Eliyahu, we just need to borrow your five hundred dollars bar mitzvah money, but by the time you are ready for Pratt, I'll have enough from the roofing business and the store. Okay, dahlink zinneleh?" Momma pleaded.

For some inexplicable reason, I gave Momma the money—anything to win her love. To make matters worse, despite my poor grades, I actually got accepted at Pratt. I was thrilled, but soon realized that Momma had no intention of paying me back. To add to my growing despair, my application to Brooklyn College—my second choice—was rejected.

It was by pure chance that I read an article about Hunter College, formerly an exclusive woman's school in the city system. Hunter was not attracting enough women and was now actively seeking male students. A sprawling campus along the reservoir awaited me in the Bronx if I could only gain admittance. Hunter looked like an Ivy League school, but fortunately for me, it wasn't. With few male applications coming in, they actually had to lower their entrance grade requirements to a C. I was immediately accepted.

The two-hour subway ride from Bensonhurst to the Bronx was not without an element of adventure. The train passed NYU and Fordham University. As I proudly wore my first Hunter College sweatshirt, I was the object of derisive whistles and catcalls from college jocks who were accustomed to seeing only women sport the Hunter insignia. In some weird way, I rather enjoyed the attention, even if they meant to mock me. The train ride also took me through Manhattan at rush hour, where the nine-to-fivers, among others, packed the subway cars, leaving standing room only. I had no problem with the crowded train since sexual groping from anonymous strangers went on daily. They would touch women, men, shopping bags, and themselves. This enhanced my fantasy life immensely.

As for my college career, I focused on my art while cheating my well-groped ass off to pass my math and science exams. Actually, I passed those classes only by sucking up to the ancient lady professors, by drawing charts and graphs, and then, after failing exams, by crying a lot. I was determined to get a B average and transfer to Brooklyn College. By the end of my first year, I had managed to earn B's in both math and science, which, along with my A's in art, gave me the average I needed to get into Brooklyn.

While my adventurous journeys to and from the Bronx were over, my days at Brooklyn College were enriching. I took several art classes and got involved in drama club productions. The contrast between exciting new experiences at college and the same old, same old at home was becoming painfully obvious. At school, my art, my designs, and my ideas were welcomed by like-minded art and theater enthusiasts. At home, nothing I did was ever noticed, let alone appreciated. Life in my parents' house became more and more unbearable. Every time I looked at the hideous green sofa and the palm leaf wallpaper, my loathing for my mother grew. Seeing Pop emasculated by her, one of the only bonds we seemed to share, just intensified my feelings.

At about that time, *The New York Times* began running a regular theater column called "Across the Tiber." I liked the name Tiber. It seemed like a non-Jewish shortening of the dreaded Teichberg name I had come to loathe. I was nearing eighteen and had read somewhere that I had the legal right to change my name. I hired a lawyer to effect the change, explaining to my parents that a shorter surname would make life easier when I hunted for a job after graduation.

"Are you meshugenah? When you go down the street, everyone knows you are a Teichberg. With that goyish name, nobody will know who you are!" Momma shrieked. Pop seemed to care less, or at least, as usual, had nothing to say on the subject.

At this point, I realized that, with or without a new name, I had no intention of spending the rest of my days on the streets of Bensonhurst. The clincher came when I read that Hunter College was opening its Manhattan Park Avenue campus to male students. A fellow student had told me that a diploma from Hunter was more impressive to prospective employers than one from Brooklyn College, so as I neared the end of my junior year, I decided to complete my degree at Hunter and move the hell out of that dreadful house!

The night before my planned exodus, I talked to my younger sister, Renee, the only person living in the house besides Momma and Pop since my older sisters' marriages. When I told Renee of my plans, she cried and begged me not to leave. I explained that it was something I had to do. Once she understood, she made me promise to come back for her as soon as possible. If there was one thing that made it hard to move out of that miserable house, it was knowing that I was leaving poor Renee alone—with them.

Early the next morning, Operation Run Like Hell swung into full gear. I had been squirreling away money by taking odd jobs, and unlike my mother, these employers actually paid me. Step one: I moved the heavy barrel of nails in the garage and carefully dislodged the two hundred dollars I had hidden there. Step two: I packed my cardboard suitcase with my pathetic collection of clothes and personal items and tied up my art portfolio. Step three: With my parents in the kitchen, far from the front door, I loudly announced, "I am moving to Manhattan!" Of course, I did this while actually standing in the doorway so that Momma couldn't block my departure.

Momma quickly entered the hallway and saw that throwing herself in front of the door was not an option. My plan was working. Within moments, she sized up the situation. Since she couldn't physically prevent me from walking out, she would try to talk me out of leaving by berating me. Momma went into her shpiel about how I would ruin my life, but I knew it couldn't get any worse than living at home. When she was done, Pop stepped around her and, looking helpless and bewildered, handed me ten dollars. Looking directly at him, I quietly said, "Thank you, Pop."

So, with two hundred and ten dollars to my name, I schlepped to the Sea Beach subway, my heart pounding with excitement and fear. Unfortunately, this is where my grand plan ended. In fact, I had no clue as to where I was going or how I would survive. I figured that if Oscar Hammerstein, Senior, father of the great composer, could leave Russia at sixteen without a penny in his pocket, find his way across the Atlantic Ocean, and become a millionaire in Manhattan, I could probably find my way across the East River to Manhattan and earn a few bucks as I completed my final year of college.

🌴 🌴 🌴

I had heard that Greenwich Village was home to artists and offered low-rent apartments for those on a modest—or, in my case, non-existent—budget. It wasn't exactly the Emerald City, but for me, it was close enough. Everything in the Village was so different from Bensonhurst. Of course, I'd never seen this part of Manhattan. Outside of Brooklyn and Hunter in the Bronx, I'd seen only the Lower East Side of the city and the sleazy theaters around Forty-Second Street and Times Square.

In the Village, age-old steepled churches, flanked by cobblestone alleys and graveyards with toppling headstones, served as landmarks along streets lined with shops, artist cafés, coffee houses, and century-old walkups. Unlike the bland windows of Bensonhurst's retail establishments, these store windows expressed the unconventional personalities of the owners. And right in the middle of it all was famed Washington Square Park, home to a large water fountain and the stately marble arch that Stanford White had modeled on the Arc de Triomphe in Paris.

During the 1950s, Washington Square had emerged as a gathering spot for artists, jewelry makers, poets, bohemians, roller skaters, chess players, and a potpourri of other creative New York residents. It was a place to exchange new ideas, to experiment with drugs and sexuality, to express oneself in poetry, in song, or in art. It was the antithesis of Bensonhurst, where everyone wore the same clothes and followed the same rigid social rules. In the Village, there was no conformity, no "right" way of doing things. This was reflected even in the streets, which were narrow and winding—so unlike the predictable straight-lined grid of Brooklyn neighborhoods.

It was 1953, and the Beat Generation—a group of writers known for their rejection of conventional social values—was starting to emerge. Jack Kerouac had already written his first jazz-influenced novel, while Village coffee houses and bars provided a stage for Allen Ginsberg and other poets of the time. Folk singers like Pete Seeger and Phil Ochs also performed in Village venues. And at the Village Gate, jazz musicians like Thelonious Monk, Miles Davis, and Anita O'Day created an exciting new sound for this new generation. There was even an annual art show held in Washington Square Park.

As I made my way down the narrow streets, I took it all in— all the colors, all the sounds, all the different people. In Brooklyn, society's rigid definition of appropriate behavior had made me feel like a perpetual outsider. The Village not only tolerated diverse lifestyle and points of view, but actually celebrated them. Here I would not have to define or explain my rapidly emerging homosexuality or justify my developing art style. There was no Momma to make me feel ugly, stupid, and inadequate. I didn't understand ninety-nine percent of the poetry being recited in the local cafés or the avant-garde plays being performed as street theater, but it really didn't matter. I was home. Now all I needed to do was find an apartment.

With my entire savings in my pocket, I strolled along Greenwich Avenue. There were quite a few "For Rent" signs, but I had no idea what an apartment might cost. Stopping at a coffee shop, I ordered what seemed to me an exotic Beatnik drink: café espresso. As I sipped the strong brew, I looked across the avenue to a five-story apartment building. Narrow, run-down, and leaning to one side, it looked very "Village" to me. Maybe it was fate, but tacked to the front door was a sign that read "Artist Studio for Rent." Leaving the café, I crossed the street and rang the super's bell.

A tall skinny man with a pasty white face came to the door. A purple cigarette dangled from his lopsided lips, and strangely sweet-smelling ashes dropped onto a scrubby shirt and a pair of pants so filthy that they seemed to have been plucked from a trash bin. It didn't matter. He had a top-floor artist studio available immediately.

I asked him about the apartment, "It's for rent for twenty-five dollars a month . . . as is!" he explained. I had no idea what "as is" meant. We trudged our way up the five flights of steep, creaky stairs. When we finally reached the top floor, straight ahead of us was an apartment with no front door. Instead, the entrance was curtained by beads interlaced with leis and tiny colorful lights. Peering inside the room, I could see naked light bulbs camouflaged by colorful garlands and more tiny Christmas bulbs. Located to my immediate left was the only other apartment on the floor, which sat behind an actual wooden door. The super led me into the one-room studio.

I was both nervous and excited as I looked over the long narrow room crammed with odds and ends. The overall space was surprisingly well lit. When I looked upwards, I saw that in the middle of the peeling ceiling was a large rectangular skylight. The glass panes may have been covered with grime, but even so, the sun managed to illuminate the space below, reminding me of the artists' garrets I had seen in so many French movies. That was a definite plus, and as I looked around the room, I realized that it may have been the only plus.

To the left of the entrance was a makeshift kitchen that seemed to be stapled to the wall. In the middle of the room was a bathtub. Coming out of the tub was a black hose that led to a door located on the back wall. When I attempted to pull the door open, I found that it was attached by the top hinge only. With great care, I opened the door to find a triangular area that included both a toilet bowl and a tiny sink. Many tenants ago, these porcelain fixtures had probably been white, but it was difficult to tell. The hose that ran from the tub was connected to the faucet of the sink, so using the toilet would clearly require a high degree of acrobatic skill.

Backing out of the bath-less bathroom, I peered down at the floor of the studio. It was filthy. Some sections were covered in linoleum, but others had a blackened hardwood surface.

I knew that this place was a disaster. If I had any common sense, I would have run for the nearest exit, and yet I didn't. There was something that fascinated me about this outlandish room. Maybe I saw it as a challenge, maybe it was hearing Momma's voice in my head calling me meshuga, or maybe I desperately wanted to call someplace home—my home.

Not at all apologetic about the appalling conditions, the super urged me to make up my mind. "You have to decide immediately," he said. "An agent has this listing and everyone wants to live in this neighborhood. The electric and heat is included. Rent is due exactly the first of the month. And no wild parties, no drugs, and no loud music after three AM."

Not knowing anyone to invite to a wild party or where to get drugs—not even having a radio or a bottle of aspirin—I dismissed the rules. They would not be a problem at this point in my life. But my head was swimming as I tried to make a decision. True, this was not my dream apartment, but it was cheap and there was no stucco to be found anywhere. The location was superb, on Greenwich Avenue, down the street from the Greenwich Cinema, where I could get my fill of movies. It was a genuine Greenwich Village artist's studio and it was miles away from Momma. So there I was with my cardboard suitcase and no idea as to where I might even look for another apartment. I stood in one spot and glanced around. I remember thinking, *I'm an artist. I can fix this place up and it will look swell.* So, I pulled twenty-five dollars from my pocket and handed it to the super.

"I don't give no receipts," said the man. "I ain't no bookkeeper. The last tenant left all his furniture so you can have it since the landlord ain't paying no garbage truck to haul it away." Unsmilingly, he gave me a key and left.

My first real home. No kvetching Momma to hound me. It badly needed a good scrubbing and disinfecting, but I loved it. One of the odds and ends left by the last tenant was a bed of sorts. I tried out the mattress that seemed nailed to a platform, and convinced myself that it wasn't all that uncomfortable. Another piece of cast-off furniture was a black sofa that had no cushions but was at least upright. There was also a dinette set and, much to my surprise, some dishes and some flatware. There were even a couple of pillows, a blanket, and a broom—abandoned, no doubt, by a Good Housekeeping Seal of Approval winner. It was glorious. It was home!

At about five o'clock, the initial excitement had pretty much worn off, and food was now uppermost on my mind. I realized that

I hadn't eaten all day and I was hungry. There was a pizza joint on the corner, so I grabbed my key and headed out the door.

By the time I had wolfed down a pie, it was dark. I climbed the five flights of stairs, flicked on the lights, and there they were: Roaches and roaches and roaches, oh my! This was something I had never seen before—certainly not in Momma's house, where even bugs wouldn't eat her awful food. Thousands of roaches scattered every which way and even began to crawl onto my feet. Terrified, I took the only logical course of action . . . I screamed hysterically. Then, turning, I rushed out of the apartment.

There, in front of me, stood a very short bronze-skinned guy in a moo moo, bedecked with jewelry and sporting a broad smile. "Hey, you okay?" he asked. "I was coming up the stairs and heard you yelling."

Stomping my feet to dislodge the last of the roaches, I replied, "Yeah, but I think I was just attacked by a million bugs. Ugh!" Feeling a little more composed, I suddenly realized that I was talking to a stranger. "Who are you?" I asked.

"I'm Loki. I live across the hall. You have been invaded by an army of roaches! Wait, I'll get some spray!" he offered in a high-pitched singsong voice.

Loki's spray was his own highly perfumed concoction. It didn't matter how it smelled; it worked! An hour later, no more bugs.

While we waited for the bugs to scatter or die, Loki filled me in on the previous tenant. "Reed McNaughton had to move out at three in the morning and was just minutes ahead of the cops when they came to get her, a real miss thing. I'm not sure exactly what she was wanted for, but it probably had something to do with her selling reefer. She was a huge, hairy, ugly thug. The traffic up and down the stairs was nerve-wracking. She never bothered me, fortunately. But as you see, she lived like a pig!" It would be many weeks before I understood that the term "miss thing" referred to a high-strung queen, and that it was not at all unusual to refer to such a person as "she."

Everything about Loki was fascinating, and I immediately sensed that we had some kind of connection. Having told me about the previous tenant, my new neighbor now filled me in on himself.

"I design and make bamboo wall hangings, flutes, and necklaces," Loki explained. "I'm working on bamboo jockstraps at the moment. Oh, and I happen to be a homosexual, just in case the rings on every finger and the red nail polish didn't give me away. What's your name?"

The fact that Loki had referred to himself as a homosexual amazed me, as I had never heard anyone use this term to describe himself. Loki's manner was seductive, yet safe and friendly. I couldn't quite figure out where Loki was from. I knew it wasn't Brooklyn. He didn't look quite Asian, yet not quite American either, and definitely not Jewish. Not wanting to appear naive or rude, I didn't ask.

"I'm Elliot Tiber," I told him. "I'm a student at Hunter. I'm majoring in art, theater, and design." I felt rather plain and boring compared to my flamboyant new friend, but he seemed interested in me, and that was a novel feeling in itself.

Loki invited me across the hall to his studio for tea and good-ies. I had just finished off a pizza, but that wasn't going to stop me from enjoying dessert. His studio was like a set for a South Seas Hollywood movie. Yards of colorful silks, bamboo panels, bamboo curtains, and bamboo furniture covered every inch of space. He had fashioned chandeliers of bamboo and miniature colored lights. I had never seen so much bamboo in one place; he must have had a bamboo tree hiding somewhere behind the decorative screens. Looking around, it was hard to believe that only a beaded curtain stood between us and a grubby apartment house hallway.

"I would be delighted to help you transform your junkyard studio into a garden of paradise, Elliot," he offered in his gentle little voice, all the while performing his own version of Salome's Dance of the Seven Veils. Loki's veils, though, were made of floral leis and bamboo shoots.

Eager to start our decorating project, Loki and I spent the next few days discarding most of the derelict items that littered my apartment. While we both fancied ourselves to be quite creative, there was little that could be done to salvage the previous tenants' belongings. Some dishes and a few pieces of furniture were saved; everything else was piled at the curb. Then we did our best to remove years of grime from the walls, floors, and windows. I borrowed a ladder from the super to reach the skylight, and was able to eliminate most of the dirt from the interior pane of glass. Because the hinges on the skylight had rusted shut, I had to climb onto the roof to clean the exterior surface.

Once the skylight had been scrubbed clean, light poured into the apartment below. Unfortunately, the sunlight served only to reveal the ghastly condition of the floors. The linoleum had to be pulled off—actually, scraped off. Thank goodness for the butter knives one of the former occupants had left behind. Of course, when the linoleum was gone, we could see that the exposed wooden floors were coated with layers of filth.

Loki took a look at the flooring and said, "I have just the thing. I'll be back in a jiff." He went to his apartment and returned with a box full of steel wool, sandpaper, and tools. "I use this to work on my bamboo," he explained. "It should do a good job on the floor."

For the next two days, Loki helped me sand and scrape the floor down. When we were finished, I couldn't believe it—the original oak slats looked terrific. Loki told me that the wood would require some stain and varnish, which we could apply later, but at that moment the apartment actually looked quite decent. Hell, it looked great!

Now it was time to decorate my new home. Because I had to make what little money I had last, my decorating budget was small, to say the least. This didn't seem to faze Loki in the slightest. He had many artist friends with unique apartments, and all seemed eager to supply colorful odds and ends to complete my little studio. Their eclectic contributions included a daybed, a few chandeliers, and a dining table with a reclaimed plywood top and bongo-drum legs. I was amazed by the generosity of these total strangers, but learned that since most of these artists had been abandoned by their families, they had joined together to form an extended family. This sense of community was something I had never seen before.

I learned a lot from Loki. For example, I discovered that the best time to visit hotel trash bins was after midnight. There, we found boxes of dishes and bed linens imprinted with names like "Waldorf Astoria" and "The Plaza." Only the best junk was good enough for Elliot and Loki.

With Loki by my side, I was soon finding treasures in the strangest places. A barber shop was installing new chairs, so I asked for one of the old ones before it was taken to the junkyard. The owner looked at me and nodded, having no clue why anyone would want a worn barber chair. A giant wooden spool used to roll up cable wires made a perfect table once it had been spruced up with a little paint. A couple of well-placed mirrors—discarded during the renovation of an old hotel—gave the studio a more spacious look.

I also found an elephant-based end table in hideous orange stripes, a practically new hammock, and a huge canvas circus poster. Loki had a close friend with a station wagon, and when he didn't need it for work, I used it to transport my acquisitions to their new home. One of my best finds was a Red Flyer wagon, like the one I had as a kid. I turned it into a planter for flowers . . . artificial ones.

I was quickly getting the knack of interior decorating and thanked Loki for getting me started. As a bonus, I had lost a few pounds in the process of loading items into the car and lugging them up five flights of stairs. Loki helped but he had a slight build, so moving all the heavier objects—the barber chair, for instance—was a sweaty process. Occasionally, Loki and I passed the super as we hauled our latest finds up the stairs. He stared and sometimes shook his head, but never commented. Apparently, as long as I was paying my rent, I was free to do just about anything I wanted to the apartment.

By the time I had finished cleaning, painting, and rearranging, I had fashioned my own unique design. When I sat on my barber chair and swiveled around, I felt at one with my vibrant new surroundings. Loki glanced around, too, and exclaimed something in another language.

"What does that mean?" I asked.

"That means, 'It looks great' in Hawaiian," replied my neighbor. And then it dawned on me: Loki was Hawaiian!

Within two weeks, my home was ready for the housewarming that Loki was determined to arrange. I had few city friends at that point, but he assured me that his guest list would make even Queen Liliuokalani jealous.

🌴　🌴　🌴

The housewarming was fabulous. Loki invited a swarm of at least fifty gay guys, as well some lesbians and a few "fag hags"—straight women who liked to hang out with gay men. With their extravagantly applied makeup, extraordinary jewelry, and brilliantly colored clothing, the partygoers looked like players from Central Casting. Of course, there were quite a few cross-dressers at our soirée, so determining the gender of some guests was a challenge. I had never seen transvestites before and was a bit nervous at first, but when several of them began to sing and dance, I was thrilled. At the turn of the century, my little living space had probably been the storage area of a one-family home. On this night, though, it was home to an out-of-the-closet crowd that was as bold and unconventional as Greenwich Village itself.

Since my gourmet skills were limited to arranging sliced cheese and olives on a plate, Loki took charge of the menu. He spent most of that day preparing a huge assortment of dips and delicacies from the Hawaiian Islands. He decorated massive platters with floating candles, leis, and exotic objects that to this day are a mystery to me. He filled glamorous punch bowls with liquid dynamite. Lastly, he arranged platters of assorted colored pills and funny looking homemade cigarettes. I was so inexperienced that I actually thought the pills were confections—some type of Hawaiian M&M—and the cigarettes were made of tobacco.

At Loki's request, I had devoted my time to painting palm trees, flowers, and abstract dancing boys on huge sheets of display paper. I then hung the playful works of art in the hallway outside my studio so that our guests would understand that they could spill into Loki's apartment as needed. Even though we were occupying the entire floor, once all the partygoers had arrived, there was no room to move. People were lying all over the furniture and the floor.

Everyone was drunk, stoned, or both. I had no experience with getting high, so I simply thought that these folks were more fun than anyone I had ever met before in my life. I could have used Momma's movie dishes now for sure, since the supply of colored paper plates quickly disappeared. No matter. No one cared.

It was my very first home and therefore my first housewarming party. I was overwhelmed, as everyone brought some kind of present for my studio. I received sequined pillows, huge decorative throws, wine glasses, and a bottle of champagne accompanied by long-stemmed champagne glasses. I had never even tasted champagne before and the result was that in quick time, I became drunk and giggly and began telling my funny stories to one and all. In fact, this was an evening of firsts. Perhaps most important, it was the very first time I saw guys openly hugging and kissing.

In the past, my experience with parties had been mostly limited to mind-numbing gatherings of Brooklyn yentas. Those events had made me want to climb out the nearest window. This time, though, I was surrounded by gay men and lesbian women, and they were funny, happy, and totally nonjudgmental about sexual preference, income, or color. Most seemed to come from different parts of the country, and like me, they had run away from home. These people actually appreciated my humor, and I loved listening to their wild and weird tales of jobs, sexual conquests, and travels. This alone would have made the party a most extraordinary event, but there was even more reason to celebrate. Since moving into the Village, I had completed a few abstract paintings and hung them on the walls of my studio apartment. Everyone who looked at my work and noticed my signature reacted with pleasure, excitement, and praise. Not one called my art work "schmutz," as Momma had done so many times over the years.

Among our flamboyant guests, I recognized a few people from television shows, while others talked about the Broadway plays in which they had appeared. Some were dancers, others were actors. A few were clothing designers and there was also a smattering of teachers and office workers. To my amazement, one was a six o'clock news anchor I had seen many times on TV! I was beginning to feel the pulse and thrill of living in the center of the world. I did not even realize that Loki had music playing in his apartment until I heard the strains of Judy Garland in the background. The record player crackled a bit, but it was unmistakably Judy and people were singing along. First it was the upbeat "Trolley Song," and then I heard the sweet melody of "The Boy Next Door," both favorite tunes from the wonderful film *Meet Me in St. Louis.* I was undeniably in a new and ideal world where everyone appreciated my beloved Judy and had even invited her to my very first party!

It was almost dawn when the last guests left amid hugs and kisses. Both apartments looked as if they'd been hit by a hurricane, but cleanup would have to wait until the next day. I hugged Loki and thanked him for my amazing "coming out" party. I then flopped onto my mattress and passed out.

I was dead asleep when the doorbell rang a short time later. It was Harlan, a twenty-something Broadway dancer and the most handsome black guy I'd ever seen. After apologizing for the intrusion, he explained that he must have dropped his keys somewhere in the apartment. We searched through the piles of used plates and cups, wine bottles and leis, and finally found his keys under a table. I could hardly take my eyes off his beautiful face and well-muscled body. My heart was beating wildly as a million thoughts raced through my head. Could I possibly suggest that he sleep over? After all, it was late and he was as drunk as I was. Then again, was there even a chance that this stunning man would be interested in an ugly Jewish boy from Bensonhurst?

Nervous and excited, I barely noticed that Harlan had begun to fill a garbage pail with paper plates and cups. He was talking to me, but I couldn't focus on anything he said. Abruptly, he stopped sifting through the party's detritus, took me in his arms, and kissed me with a passion I didn't know existed. I was all over him in what I later came to know as a "New York minute"!

I had made love before, but never had it affected me so powerfully. Maybe it was my newfound freedom; maybe it was knowing that I wouldn't have to face Momma in the morning. Whatever the reason, the night I spent with Harlan was totally engulfing. We slept until late in the afternoon and were awakened by Loki, who crept into the apartment wearing a moo moo and carrying a tray of coffee and Bromo Seltzer.

🌴 🌴 🌴

Finding my first apartment and throwing my first real party were now behind me. I settled into the neighborhood and set out by subway to register for my first classes at Hunter College in uptown Manhattan. This was not at all like the sprawling Bronx campus I had known, but consisted of several buildings interspersed with midtown offices and apartment houses. I didn't care because they had a huge art department. Math and science were still a mystery to me, but my art classes were an endless joy.

I used my subway travel time to study so that I could fit in the part-time jobs needed to pay college tuition and living expenses. Occasionally, I phoned my father to see how things were going and to let him know what I was doing. It was always a lopsided conversation, with me talking and him grunting in response. However, I was the dutiful son. He, in turn, secretly sent me fifty dollars a month to cover my rent and a few extras. I figured that if a month went by without his sending the money, I'd know that Momma had discovered what he was doing and killed him. Fortunately for both of us, she didn't, and the money kept on coming.

Hunter had a student employment office that was able to get me a sales position in a Greenwich Village shop that sold dull businessmen's shirts and ties. I had to dress the part, but the owner let me have a box of water-damaged ties from the storage basement. This, in turn, led to another moneymaking endeavor. My friend Pom Pom (probably not his real name) was an entrepreneurial artist who sketched tourists while wearing paper jeans held together with colored tapes and laces. His outfit always drew both attention and customers. Pom Pom was kind enough to show me how to use the damaged ties to create decorative hangings, which could then be sold from a card table in the Washington Square art markets. This was an easy way to make a few bucks while watching the bizarre goings-on in the park.

I also worked as an usher in the Greenwich Cinema, down the block from my apartment. This was a plum job as I actually got paid to watch movies. I even liked the way I looked in the spiffy maroon uniform. A couple of times a week, my first business mentor, Pom Pom, and a few of his friends would come by and I'd let them in through an exit door. I loved it all. Pom Pom would throw lots of parties at his place, and I would help serve food and drinks while enjoying the exciting show biz chatter. Some of Pom Pom's pals even provided comped tickets for dance performances at local storefront theaters and the City Center, a world-famous theater in midtown Manhattan.

Since my exodus from Bensonhurst twelve months before, my life had changed immeasurably. As graduation from Hunter College approached, I knew that I wanted to begin my career as an artist as soon as possible. Since I was going to graduate in June, I requested that Professor Hechtman, my college advisor, allow me to complete the entire term's assignments by April, two months before the rest of the class turned in their work. This would give me a head start in my job search. I would hand in my final assignments early, and if I got a job, I would receive attendance credit for the two months of classes I missed.

Looking back, I am truly amazed by my naiveté. Between my teacher's blessings and my success in college courses, I thought I had it made. In reality, my portfolio was a conglomeration of paintings, promotional designs, and fashion layouts, all of which had been completed as homework assignments. Compared with the professional portfolios of Pratt Institute students, mine was a joke. Of course, I didn't know that at the time. I was ready to conquer the world. I got a haircut and bought a fashionable Pierre Cardin suit and a shiny black artist portfolio. Dousing myself with Old Spice cologne, I then set out on my job-seeking mission.

My first stop was the student employment office at Hunter, where I spoke to Miss Henrietta Rittenberg. A small woman in her seventies, she had dentures and red hair that seemed, well, just wrong on a lady of that age. Nevertheless, she was in charge of graduate job placement, so I confidently presented her with my portfolio.

"Good thing you took typing classes," was Miss Rittenberg's response. "Nobody in advertising, fashion, or interior decorating will hire you. But I don't want you to take it personally. Our art students never get jobs in the fields they want. The best I can suggest is that you get a job as a typist, maybe in an ad agency. That will at least get you inside." These were her words of encouragement.

"Why didn't the art department faculty know this? Why didn't they tell me?" I asked, hoping for some better news.

"The art faculty are a bunch of Beatniks, failed artists, and designers who have tenure and steady health plans," she laughed. "Better keep practicing your typing, Elliot," she said, as bits of her afternoon snack tap-danced across her dentures.

Where was this coming from? I wondered. I was reasonably sure that Miss Rittenberg had spoken to Momma. I was very aware that nearly all aspiring painters couldn't make a living, let alone find a gallery that would show their work. While attending Brooklyn College, I had witnessed the frustration of Mark Rothko and Ad Rheinhardt, instructors who had tried unsuccessfully to make their mark in the art world. I had crossed becoming a painter off my list early on, but this was *commercial* art.

In spite of Rittenberg's prediction of doom, or maybe because of it, I was now determined to complete all my assignments and break into the field of design. In fact, I now had two people to prove wrong. Of course, I would have to work fast since neither Momma nor Miss Rittenberg was getting any younger.

4

Elliot Tiber, Decorator

My graduation from Hunter College would involve no pomp, and the only circumstance was my need for an immediate job. So I finished my class work by the end of April, as agreed upon with my professors, and didn't even attend the ceremony. My diploma arrived by mail and the only person disappointed by this turn of events was my younger sister, Renee. I had promised that after the ceremony, she would get all the ice cream she could eat at Junior's, a popular Brooklyn eatery that was famous for desserts. A bit let down, she and her friends went to Junior's anyway and ordered at least ten flavors with every topping imaginable. In retrospect, the graduation ceremony, with family present, probably would have been an embarrassment, with Momma jumping up as soon as they announced "Elliot Tiber" and bellowing, "It's *Teichberg*! His real name is *Teichberg*!"

So, armed with my portfolio and wearing my Pierre Cardin suit, I began my job search by approaching several art agencies. After the third art director's unenthusiastic response to my portfolio, it was clear that I was wasting everyone's time by offering an amateurish assortment of fashion, textiles, lettering, interior decorating, and theater set designs, none of which would get me any legitimate work in an advertising or art agency. Henrietta Rittenberg had been right; my classical art professors at Hunter had no clue as to what passed for commercial design in the real world. While Hunter College was not a bad school, it was no Pratt or Cooper Union.

My next option was to look for work in department stores. I'd seen enough Manhattan store windows to know that they needed some fresh ideas. At first, I answered ads from any large store that was looking for an artist of any kind. Nothing. Then I started to walk into any large store that I happened to pass. A few days into my search, I wandered into W. & J. Sloane on Fifth Avenue. From the street it had looked like a department store, but it was actually a furniture and decorating emporium that had been established in the mid-1800s by William and John Sloane. Fortunately, I wandered the floors before inquiring about a job, as it was only after seeing endless aisles of tables, chairs, and sofas that I realized what this famous Manhattan store was selling.

A sympathetic salesman suggested that I try the display department rather than the interior decorating division. On my way, I passed through a black-painted maze of crystal chandeliers, bolts of fabric, huge rolls of colored background paper, and shelves packed with chachkas. At the end of this Alice-in-Wonderland passage was an office covered in flocked fleur-de-lis wallpaper with a massive gold French desk at its center. There on an ornately carved gold chair sat department manager Gregory Rossov, a Russian expatriate. With a welcoming smile, Mr. Rossov motioned me to sit down on a Napoleon campaign chair. His right hand, adorned with a multitude of rings, clutched a generously sized glass of brandy, while a crystal ashtray held a recently lit black-and-gold cigarette. Rossov's suit was an elegant pin-striped affair, though much too tight. The neck of the jacket sported a wide ascot, and the sleeves ended in huge diamond cufflinks. This was a sight like none I had ever seen. Certainly no one in Brooklyn ever dressed like this.

Mr. Rossov greeted me and asked if I were applying for the display job. Having just wandered in off the street, I didn't know that there was a "display job" available, but of course, I replied in the affirmative. I then placed my pathetic portfolio on his desk and opened it for examination. As he perused my offerings, he spilled some of his brandy on my portfolio. Seeing my alarm, Rossov rose to his feet, staggered to my chair, and wrapped an arm around my shoulder. "It's wonderful," he enthused. "You have the kind of talent Sloane's needs. You're hired! When can you start?"

I was thrilled and offered to begin as soon as possible. I had landed my first job! My only concern was that when I showed up for work, Rossov, then sober, would not remember hiring me. Nonetheless, I immediately called Momma with the big news.

"Momma! I got a job at W. J. Sloane's on Fifth Avenue! I begin tomorrow!" I screamed into the phone.

"What's Sloane's? Yonkel, Elli got a job on Fifth Avenue. Teichberg's Housewares Store isn't good enough for him, I guess. Fifth Avenue is better than Twentieth Avenue!"

"My boss is Russian. Mr. Rossov!"

"Rossov? Doesn't sound Jewish. It's no good. You never were any good, Elli. When you lose that rotten job, don't come running back to Twentieth Avenue!" She hung up.

I then phoned Professor Hechtman and Edna Luetz, the chair of Hunter's Art Department. They seemed genuinely thrilled by the news. I figured they were thinking, "Finally, one of our students got a design job. Who would have thought?"

Showing up bright and early the next morning, I honestly didn't know what I was expected to do. Mr. Rossov's assistant introduced me to Ryan Lotto, who was in charge of the Fifth Avenue windows and was supposed to show me how things worked at Sloane's. Ryan explained that in a few days, we were going to install five new window displays overnight, as the store did not permit work on the windows during daytime shopping hours. In the meantime, we would assemble the merchandise that would make up the displays.

In the days that followed, staff members dragged assorted furniture and decorative items into a holding area from which we would draw the display merchandise. Ryan, who was always somewhat drunk, took some time to show me the miracle invention of the era, the staple gun. *Nothing like a drunk armed with a staple gun,* I thought as I stationed myself at a safe distance from Ryan's gun-wielding hand.

Mr. Rossov then arrived and declared, "Ryan dahlink. Display is temporary. Staple everything. It's only for a month, not forever! Elliot? Ryan will show you everything you need to know. Just make sure to put a vase of white roses in each window." He sauntered off to places unknown, probably in search of more brandy.

The big night arrived. We were to work as late as necessary aided by a staff of carpenters, electricians, and other handymen. After rolling down giant shades to shield the windows from public view, we put together the walls of a studio, a bedroom, a dining room, a den, and a garden full of white roses. It was exhilarating for me but exhausting for Ryan, who had been doing this for several years while swigging booze.

Somewhere around ten in the evening, Ryan decided that he had to sleep and stretched out on a lavish bed in one of the aisles. The workmen did not seem surprised, but looked to me for further direction. I had no idea which items were supposed to go in each display. Never in my life had I seen such a collection of chairs, tables, couches, and oriental rugs, not to mention all the art objects that were to be featured in the windows.

I rushed down to Mr. Rossov's office. He was fast asleep on a recliner, an empty champagne bottle on the floor near his feet. I hesitated, but decided that I'd rather wake him than make a mess of the job.

"Excuse me, Mr. Rossov. Mr. Rossov . . . Ryan, uh, doesn't seem to be well. He's a little out of commission. There are a dozen work-men waiting for instructions. Ryan built the walls and stapled wall-paper up and hung lights, but then he had to lie down on one of the display beds. What should I do now?" I pleaded.

Gregory awoke, looked at me, and grinned. "Just make it all look like opening night at the Metropolitan Opera or Broadway. You have such exquisite taste, I'm sure it will be wonderful." With that, he shut his eyes and returned to a deep sleep.

For the next several panic-filled hours—which seemed like days—I had the workmen load each of the window displays with furnishings selected from both the holding area and the aisles. I used my sense of proportion, color, and design to compose rooms that would capture the attention of window shoppers while show-casing the store's merchandise. I don't know how I functioned in that chaos. My many attempts to revive Ryan were futile. Finally, when it was time to complete the model bedroom, the workmen yanked Ryan out of the bed, assuming that customers would find the furniture more appealing if it wasn't occupied by a loudly snoring drunk.

The next morning, we rolled up the shades at nine o'clock to find Mr. Rossov standing on the sidewalk beside Sloane's CEO. The two men moved from window to window as Ryan and I stood nearby, trying to hear their comments. All I could think was, *Do I still have a job?*

"Gregory, you have outdone yourself!" the CEO exclaimed. "These windows are the ultimate statement of Sloane's taste. Congratulations!"

Speaking in a conspiratorial whisper, Ryan commented, "The boss doesn't know shit, but I'm glad he likes it. Now maybe he'll leave me alone and Rossov will be after you for his intimate dinners!"

I was elated. My first Fifth Avenue windows were a stunning success! Now I just wanted to go home and sleep. As I changed my clothes in the locker room, Mr. Rossov entered and asked me to meet him in his office. Ryan giggled, spilling beer onto his already stained work shirt.

Mr. Rossov leaned back in his chair, smiling. "You passed your test," he said. "Congratulations, Elliot. I'm delighted to make you a permanent addition to our staff."

"My test?" I asked. "Was Ryan part of the test?"

"Well, yes and no. I know Ryan, and it was likely he wanted to see how good you are. I certainly couldn't hire you until you proved yourself. You did a wonderful job! Was this your first job in window display?"

"I did the displays in my parents' store in Brooklyn since I was a kid," I explained. I then added, "My mother is from Russia, too. From Belorussia."

"Nothing but peasants in Belorussia," Rossov sneered. "I was fortieth in line to the Czar, but the peasants had their revolution and ended all that. So I am reduced to working for a living. But I won't hold that against you. You must come over to my apartment to celebrate. We'll have an intimate dinner for two."

Still floating on air, I said "Yes, Mr. Rossov. I would love to come over." *How does he know that Momma was a peasant?* I wondered.

🌴 🌴 🌴

I had never been in a ten-room Central Park South apartment, and when Rossov greeted me at the door, I was a bit overwhelmed. The ornate entry hall alone was bigger than my entire Village apartment. The walls were covered with silk burgundy wallpaper trimmed by gold-leafed moldings. The ceilings were at least fifteen feet high. The enormous dining room held a richly carved table that could seat at least sixteen people beneath its shining gold candelabra. The red wood library overflowed with leather-bound antique books. Wherever you looked, cherubs danced on ceilings, walls, and furnishings. Wherever you walked, you trod on richly hued oriental rugs.

Rossov showed me to a large marble bathroom and told me to take a shower. The bathroom offered an assortment of floor-length robes, and after showering, I chose one made of black velvet with woven cherubs. I then went in search of my host.

After glancing in several rooms, I found Rossov in the master bedroom, a silk-covered Renaissance-style room that held the biggest bed I had ever seen. My host, clad in a Chinese emperor's robe, was totally looped. He informed me that he wore a real Ming

Dynasty garment. In art history, I had studied the Ming Dynasty, so I at least knew what he was referring to. However, in no art class had they shown us robes, and certainly not ones worn by overweight, middle-aged, drunken Russians.

"My wife is away traveling, so we are alone," he explained, pointing to a wedding picture in an ornate frame by the bed. He then motioned for me to join him on the bed, but I stood there, frozen. Was this what Ryan had meant when he said that Rossov would now be after me? If only my host had worn a black leather motorcycle jacket, I might have gotten aroused. No matter, because as he fumbled to open his Ming Dynasty robe, he passed out. I found a guest bedroom and went to sleep, relieved and exhausted.

The next morning, Rossov remembered nothing of the previous night. "Dahlink, you were divine last night. And don't concern yourself with our age difference. I am only fifty, barely double your age. But you are quite mature!" It seems that my sexual performance, or lack thereof, had made a wonderful impression. I had passed my second test.

For the next six months, Sloane's would be my home, and window displays would be my artistic form of expression. Rossov must have found other house guests because he no longer invited me to his lavish apartment. As I continued working, I started using some of my own paintings to decorate the model rooms. I had years of artwork at my disposal, including Rothko-style abstracts and Picasso-style women with a bit of romanticism of my own invention. It was usual for customers to order not only complete rooms of furniture, exactly as seen in the windows, but also all the rugs, lamps, and paintings featured in the display. So in addition to my salary, I made money by selling my paintings to Sloane's. They would buy the art at a wholesale price and then mark it up and sell it.

Of course, I once again pushed my luck by calling Momma and inviting her, Pop, and my sisters into the city to see my windows and my art. "Yonkel? Elli wants us to come to the city to see his windows and paintings. Maybe we should go before they fire him because he doesn't know what he is doing!" she hollered.

To my complete surprise, one Sunday, my parents called to tell me they were coming to see the windows. I was glad it was a Sunday and that Rossov would not be there. I'm pretty sure my mother's take on Russian nobility would have been much like Mr. Rossov's on peasantry. My three sisters stood on the sidewalk, staring in awe at the displays of furnishings behind the large panes of glass. Goldie was thrilled to discover that my paintings were included in each of the five windows. She always had a passion for art and knew how difficult it was to win any type of recognition in the field. Dad looked quite proud. Momma simply grimaced. What did I expect?

"Only goys would buy such things. Who are the women in those pictures? Why didn't you paint mine picture or at least one of your sisters?" Yes, I'm sure a portrait of my mother, yelling, would have brightened up any display window. As Momma stomped back to the car, she suggested that we all head down to Ratner's, our favorite Jewish eatery on the Lower East Side, for dinner. Meanwhile, Pop whispered, "You did a wonderful job, boychick."

"Congratulations, Elli. I had no idea you knew how to do this," Goldie offered.

Rachelle and Renee—unable to give hugs, of course—told me how beautiful they thought the windows were, and let me know that they were very proud.

For the first time, my life was taking shape on my own terms. This was the beginning of my decorating career, and despite

Momma's opinion, my work was being accepted and appreciated, and I was getting paid for it. There was no question about it—dinner at Ratner's would be on me.

🌴 🌴 🌴

The summer before I began working at Sloane's, my parents had decided to take a vacation. It was something they had never done, at least not since I was born. I guess it was long overdue. It had been a swelteringly hot summer, and I figured I could use a few days off. Just as important, Renee had begged me to join them on their getaway.

"El, we've never been to the country. We've never even seen a lake! You're so busy all the time that I hardly ever get to spend time with you, and you can certainly use a break," she said. "Don't you want to see Momma and Poppa on vacation?" Whatever the reason, I agreed to go.

We stayed at Pauline's Rooming House in White Lake, New York, and what began as a weekend, turned into a week. It was interesting to see my parents in "vacation mode." Momma was actually going into the water instead of standing at a cash register. Dad was lying on a lounge chair instead of a roof. They weren't even fighting. It was indeed surreal and a bit unnerving.

Of course, Momma's enterprising mind was always at work, and she was quite impressed that all of Pauline's twenty Depression-era rooms were full. With very few other hotels or even bed and breakfasts in the area, she began contemplating the possibility of making money as the owner of such an establishment. As luck would have it (bad luck, actually), there was an empty Victorian rooming house down the road. Momma made inquiries about who owned it and what they were asking for it, and when she learned about the rock-bottom price, presto, she made arrangements to buy it!

My folks were suddenly convinced that the following summer, they would become the next Grossingers—the family that owned one of the most celebrated hotels in all of the Catskills. Thankfully, my parents did not decide to name their new establishment Teichbergs. The fact that there were few motels and hotels around White Lake was possibly a sign that, not unlike Siberia, this was not a popular tourist stop. The former grand hotels that had once stood in the area were mostly abandoned, and the few that still operated survived solely because of their old customers—and by "old," I don't mean just "long-time." The Catskills area was still thriving, with several major hotels packing in the Jewish clientele who wanted to escape the heat of the city. But this was not the Catskills; this was White Lake, and the Teichbergs not only weren't the Grossingers, but also didn't know how to run a hotel. In fact, it wouldn't be long until my parents demonstrated that they were equally adept at running a hotel as they were at parenting. Oy!

In the ensuing months—actually, throughout the entire winter—my folks held the sale of the century in Bensonhurst. Yes, Momma was selling everything in the store. Technically, it wasn't really a sale since none of the items were marked with prices. Instead, Momma made up prices on the spot as she always had. Although the goal was to empty the store, Momma kept ordering more and more housewares, so when she finally sold the store itself, tons of merchandise had to be packed and schlepped away. Added to this was thirty years of possessions from the stucco house, which was cleared out from attic to basement. Momma and Poppa felt that between the sale of the store, the building that included the store, and the house, they would not only cover the cost of their dream hotel, but also have enough money to fix it up and maintain it.

Once everything had been loaded into a tractor trailer, Momma and Pop headed up to White Lake. Their new property had a barn, which would become the new home of my father's roofing business, while the rooms of the house would be rented to guests.

The next summer, my parents began running what they believed to be a motel. I say "believed to be" because few people who stopped there ever actually agreed with them. Nonetheless, Pop converted the Victorian's six rooms into nine rentable rooms with one shared bathroom. In an effort to be the dutiful son, I pitched in and helped them fix up the motel from hell. For some inexplicable reason, I wanted to be supportive, certainly not for Momma's sake but perhaps because Pop had been sending me money, so in his own way, he had been supportive of me. Or perhaps it was just my way of trying to forget that I had not yet found someone significant with whom I could spend my weekends.

🌴 🌴 🌴

Once Momma and Pop moved to White Lake, my dual life began. I spent summer weekends out in the shabby motel, while my weekdays, year round, were spent working in the city. Renee got her first of many secretarial jobs and a tiny studio apartment on the West Side, so she was nearby.

My career was also undergoing changes. One of the executives at B. Altman and Company, a well-respected Manhattan department store, saw my windows at Sloane's and offered me twice the salary. For a hundred dollars a week, I started out as a staff artist, and very quickly, I was promoted to art director. No additional pay, but an impressive title. The problem was, I hated B. Altman's. Its reputation of conservatism was reflected in both its staid approach to window displays and its merchandise. As a result, I had no creative freedom and was bored to death.

The B. Altman's cloud had a silver lining, though. One of the design firms used by the store had a Greenwich Village factory where they did some of the most innovative, imaginative work in the country. I got to know the president and finally gathered enough chutzpah to ask him for a job. He immediately hired me at the same hundred dollars a week I was getting from B. Altman's. I didn't care about the money; I simply wanted to enjoy what I was doing.

Although I loved my new job, my pattern of constantly switching companies had officially begun. Within the next few months, I was courted by several design firms, all of which offered good pay for the fun of creating imaginative in-store displays. I changed jobs two more times and got to see my designs featured in Lord & Taylor, Bloomingdale's, Macy's, Neiman Marcus, and other big-name establishments nationwide. It was heaven. During this time, I told Pop that he could stop sending me money every month. In just over a year, I had become self-sufficient—almost. At any rate, I had taken a giant step in my life, and I knew it.

Like my parents, I possessed a strong entrepreneurial spirit and wanted to have my own business, so I opened Plaza Interiors. Momma, ever critical, suggested, "You should call it 'Teichberg Interiors.' No one will want to work with Plaza Interiors. If people know you are a Teichberg, you might make money."

Actually, to launch my new enterprise, I didn't do much more than place some small classified ads in *The New York Times*. I included the name of my company, Plaza Interiors, and mentioned that I was formerly of W. & J. Sloane and B. Altman's. The ads included my home phone number and requested that the reader call after six in the evening. I really didn't know what to expect, if anything, until I received a call from a senior telephone company executive very much in need of an interior decorator.

"Hello Elliot," said Christina. "My husband, Ronald, and I would like to have a stunning apartment. After thirty-five years of marriage and living with the same old furnishings our parents gave us, we'd like you to come up with something special. Could you do that for us, my dear?" Christina requested. And so I did.

Although Christina had expressed the need for a change, I was surprised that she and her husband approved of everything I suggested, from the shocking pink living room to the purple-and-silver bedroom and the black lacquered kitchen. Of course, there was also my mural; I always painted a mural. The couple was obviously quite wealthy and more than happy to let me make the decisions while they paid the bills.

Ronald and Christina were just the first of many calls I received in response to my ads. Unfortunately, the calls did not come frequently enough to permit me to quit my new day job, which was at Detroit Furniture, a Brooklyn-based outfit that had nothing at all to do with Detroit. What impressed me most was that the firm offered me two hundred dollars a week, which was twice my weekly salary at the time. I couldn't say no.

🌴 🌴 🌴

Considering my new job and the additional income generated by Plaza Interiors, I thought it was time to upgrade my living quarters.

I wandered past the Village's cafés, antique shops, and bohemian boutiques until I noticed an "Apartment for Rent" sign affixed to a high rise on Sheridan Square. From there, it was a short stroll to Christopher Street, where many gay bars were located. It was also a stone's throw from Seventh Avenue South, a center of gay and lesbian life. Maybe this was the place I'd find Mr. Right.

The building manager showed me a one-bedroom penthouse apartment with a breathtaking view of the Village. It even had a dishwasher, which was a real rarity. The monthly rent was sixty dollars—the going rate for luxury apartments—and in exchange for three months' rent in cash, he agreed to fast-track my application so I could move in the next day.

Because I had completed so many interior decorating jobs by then, I knew the ins and outs of buying furnishings. I also had connections with plenty of furniture showrooms, many of which would charge me bargain prices and provide immediate delivery. I decided to let Loki have most of my old stuff and move only a few essentials, such as the barber chair and, of course, my own creations.

At the time, the mecca for interior designers was Third Avenue's Decoration & Design Building, or D&D Building, which included eighteen floors of showrooms. I rushed over to Third Avenue and bought discontinued floor samples, lamps, tables, drapes, and accessories that I could have trucked the next day. Because this was Manhattan, there was a mattress store, a linen shop, and a lighting boutique all within a five-minute walk. By ten o'clock the next evening, I was in my new home—a real New York City apartment. I had a bed to sleep in, a full living room, even a coffee pot and new towels. I was miffed that I couldn't get a telephone installed or a television hooked up for another few days, but I felt I had done pretty well in a short space of time.

Within two weeks, my Sheridan Square apartment had become a kaleidoscope of design periods and, of course, colors. My favorite colors were black and fuchsia, so I had the handyman paint the entry hall and bedroom fuchsia, and the living room all black—and by this I mean that the walls, ceilings, carpeting, and even the furniture were black. I lined drawers with the damask wallpaper samples I had collected from my decorating jobs. I did it for clients, so I was certainly going to do it for my own home. I picked up some used theatrical spotlights and focused them dramatically, creating a Broadway show look mixed with a bit of Coney Island Steeplechase Park and a touch of Paris bordello. I travelled to the Bowery to find companies that supplied restaurants, and there I bought drinking glasses, hot pink tablecloths, purple napkins, and an old-fashioned bar. The bar was much too big, but I fell in love with it and decided that I'd somehow make it fit. For the first time, I was my own client, and I was determined to please my own unique sense of taste.

Once my apartment had been fully furnished and decorated, I started going out to Village pubs and cafés. There, I made new friends, both gay and straight. While my apartment was not especially large, it was certainly more spacious than my last one and was perfect for parties—lots of parties. The parties would serve two purposes. First, they would be a great way to finally meet a decent boyfriend. Second, while the newspaper ads were bringing in some business, I suspected that the parties would be a more effective means of attracting potential clients. My black walls were just right for displaying my art. I loved painting so much that I would often stay up all hours working and reworking my canvases, even if I had to go to a job the next morning. While I painted, I always listened to Bach, Verdi, or Mozart, mixed, of course, with my Judy Garland collection. While the great composers were marvelous background music, Judy's voice always inspired me to try something new and different.

I made a habit of throwing parties almost every month, inviting an array of interesting people and telling them to bring along their own friends, as well. The resulting mix of guests ranged from deranged drag queens, cross-dressing lesbians, and leather lovers to straight artists and carefully selected clients, who seemed delighted to attend what they considered a "cutting edge New York party." My gatherings gave clients something to tell their friends about, which, in turn, brought in more customers. While my parents were never on the guest list, my kid sister, Renee, came to many of my parties and fully enjoyed herself. I was happy to have her participate in my life away from Brooklyn. At first, I insisted on re-dressing her for my soirées. I felt that her usual solid-citizen clothing wouldn't do, so I added a feather boa here and a sequined jacket there. But I could see that Renee wasn't very comfortable in what she regarded as a costume, so I eventually had to accept her own choices.

Many of my theatrical acquaintances tried to get Renee to provide tidbits of information about my past, but she understood that I had no desire to rehash old times with new friends. I preferred to have an air of mystery and let others fill in the blanks; it was a lot more fun. I hosted these parties for about a year. Since I absolutely never found a Mr. Right among all those Mr. Wrongs, I stopped. I did, however, manage to collect a huge number of friends and to expand my business, as well.

Occasionally, I had lunch with one of my former Hunter professors, Anna McKenna, and at one meal, I mentioned my parties to her. I never thought she'd attend, but she did, and was impressed with the paintings I had produced during my short post-Hunter career. From our lunchtime conversations, Anna knew that I wanted to turn Plaza Interiors into a full-time business, but that I would require a steady base of clients to do so. She also knew that big-name clients meant a lot in the decorating business. It was as much about whose house you decorated as it was about the work you did. She told me that she had given a young opera singer, Marguerite Piazza, a place to stay when she was first studying in New York City. Now, Marguerite was a big star at the Metropolitan Opera and was also featured on the popular TV variety series *Your Show of Shows*. Wow. Anna arranged a meeting.

Marguerite was both beautiful and charming. I asked if she would allow me to design a model morning room in her name for the upcoming National Antiques Show, which was being arranged by the National Society of Interior Decorators (NSID) at the New York Coliseum. As a means of drawing attention to this already prestigious event, the show was going to include some celebrities in their own "rooms." The NSID was the most respected group of decorators in the country, so this could be a major step toward expanding Plaza Interiors. I was thrilled when Marguerite said yes.

The sitting room I created for the show won rave reviews and immediately made me a "prominent NSID designer." It was at this same event that I became friendly with designer Curtis Murray. Very, very gay with a superb sense of humor, Curtis had no formal training, but was a boy toy of a diamond dealer in Paris. He had picked up French through his boyfriend, but his classic sense of style was his own.

Curtis was decorating Barbra Streisand's apartment and hired me to help shop for antiques. These excursions proved to be invaluable because it was through them that I discovered novel ways to pick up quality furnishings for little or no money. For instance, I learned that the trash piles around Sutton Place, a small area of affluent homes on Manhattan's Upper East Side, were a wonderful source of finds. On one occasion, Curtis and I rented a U-Haul truck and showed up at five in the morning to rescue Tiffany lampshades that someone had discarded simply because they weren't in vogue. The Salvation Army also offered surprisingly fine furnishings from time to time. When elderly tenants in exclusive buildings passed away, their kids often didn't know what to do with their parents' furniture, so they would simply donate it to the Salvation Army. Some of the items were quite nice and potentially valuable, as long as you were willing to put in a little work. Whatever we found—Victorian rocking chairs, inlay tables, chests of drawers, sofas—was carted to Curtis's work rooms, where he would clean them up and refinish or reupholster them. He had learned all about antique prints, paintings, and furniture, so he knew how to restore them, date them, and set prices—usually, exorbitant prices. I learned how to do the exact same thing for my own clients. It was not cheating; it was being inventive. And quite obviously, it made the clients happy, which was proven by the fact that they were more than willing to pay their bills. While I received little money for the work I did with Curtis, the knowledge I gleaned would benefit me for years to come.

Of course, once I had learned the tricks of antique hunting, I started accumulating higher-quality items for my own home. Over a short period of time, my apartment took on the appearance of an antique showroom as tables overflowed with stained-glass lamps, and French antique cabinets vied for space with elaborately carved sideboards—all the furnishings normally associated with living beyond one's means.

Right about this time, I received a phone call from Hunter College. Professor Hechtman, my former teacher, had suddenly come down with pneumonia, and the college was in urgent need of a replacement. My name had come up at a department meeting and they hoped that I was willing to cover the professor's classes. I could use the extra income, minimal though it was, and I figured that I couldn't do much harm to the next generation of art students during this short period of time. Certainly, I was flattered by the offer. I had graduated from Hunter only two years before, and here I was, being asked to teach! With a little bit of effort, I was able to arrange my work schedule around two afternoon classes each week.

Out of habit, I called my parents to tell them about the job. "Hi, Momma," I said when my mother picked up the phone.

"Who is it?" she demanded.

"It's me, Elliot. I just wanted to let you know that I just accepted a position at Hunter College to teach art." Silence. "Did you hear me, Momma? I'm going to teach at Hunter, my old school." Again, silence. "Ma, you okay?"

For the first time in my life, my mother was speechless. It turned out that Momma was thrilled. Sure, my decorating and design work was prominently featured in major department stores, but she had never approved of or understood either my painting or my interior decorating. Teaching a college course was entirely different. If her fat, ugly son couldn't be a rabbi, a doctor, or even a dentist, at least he could be an art professor. That she understood!

🌴 🌴 🌴

My "side" jobs—painting, decorating, and teaching—provided more money, but didn't enable me to give up my position at Detroit

Furniture. Truth be told, the Detroit job was too good to quit since it paid twice as much as B. Altman's. I had been hired to design floor and window displays for cheap knockoffs of higher-priced furnishings. If this was how they furnished apartments in Detroit, I knew I would never move there. Nonetheless, while the furniture was essentially imitations, the weekly paycheck was quite real.

My plan hadn't changed, though. I would save up my money until I could quit my day job and focus my attention solely on Plaza Interiors. I was actually feeling good about myself and hopeful about my future. And then the phone rang.

It was Renee. She had recently met the man of her dreams, and they were already engaged. It seems that they had visited our parents up at White Lake the previous Saturday, and Renee's fiancé, a salesman named George Feldman, had sold them on the idea of buying the bungalow colony next to their already struggling motel. *Sure, why not expand and have more empty rooms?*, I thought. While I adored Renee, I wasn't crazy about George's idea. Renee assured me, though, that George had many clients and contacts who would love nothing more than visiting a weekend summer retreat. George had promised that the place would be filled every weekend.

I was not nearly as confident as George because I knew who would be running this summer getaway—my parents. I was, however, happy that Renee had given me a heads-up on the Teichbergs' latest moneymaking venture. Armed with my newly gained knowledge, I would provide Momma and Pop with a much-needed dose of reality.

The following day, before I could even call my parents, the phone rang again. It was Momma.

"Elliot dahlink, guess what?"

"You bought a bungalow colony and proved beyond the shadow of a doubt that you are out of your mind," was my response.

"How did you know?" asked Momma.

While that was a great opening for any of a thousand comeback lines, I was smart enough to avoid a smart-ass answer. Then Momma hit me with something totally unexpected.

"Elliot, now that you are teaching and doing so well, we want you to come into business with us!"

"No, Momma, I have a business . . . Plaza Interiors." I tried to enunciate clearly so that there would be no mistake about what I was saying.

"No, you don't understand, this is a real business. These are bungalows, people can rent them, they're very nice."

"I know what bungalows are, Momma, and I can help you paint them, but I don't want to go into business with you and Pop."

"What, you don't want to help your parents? You're teaching so now you're too good for us? We gave you food, clothing, a job in the store, a roof over your head, and this is how you thank us?" As usual, Momma felt she could win me over by reminding me of my glorious childhood.

"Momma, it's not that, it's just that. . . ." She didn't let me finish. She was on a roll.

"At least you could come up and cosign at the bank so we can get a mortgage. Is that too much to ask of our only son? You just have to sign a piece of paper. You meet the banker, he's not Jewish but he's a mensch. Then you sign. You can't do that for your only parents?"

There it was, the real reason for this sudden partnership idea. My parents, already strapped by their first mortgage and the expense of maintaining one motel, had overextended themselves.

Now they needed me to cosign their new mortgage. Momma pleaded with me and in the end, I caved.

I took the following Friday off and drove upstate to the motel. I knew better than to get involved, but I just couldn't say no. When we got to the bank, bad became worse. According to the banker, before I cosigned for a loan, I was required to have an interest in the business. In other words, I had to become a partner in the bungalow colony. As I signed document after document for my parents' property, called the "El Borrio," I knew it was a mistake, but somehow, I couldn't make myself stand up and walk out as I had done several years before in Bensonhurst.

As we left the bank, Momma pointed out, "Now that we gave you a piece of the business, you can tell all your friends to come to our motel." I was still numb. "For now," she continued, "you can help us fix up the place, fancy schmancy."

At that moment, I realized that I was not only on the hook for the loan, but was also expected to turn the property into the Taj Mahal, or at least make it presentable. So much for leaving my position at Detroit Furniture. I would have felt better just throwing the money directly into White Lake. Instead, I was going to slowly funnel both my cash and my energy into a very bad scheme.

I remember that weekend well. After spending Friday signing my life away to bankers, I spent Saturday and Sunday helping my parents, Renee, and George clean up a dozen bungalows. Wiping away an occasional tear, I wondered exactly how it had happened. Why had I done this? How had they suckered me in? I had succumbed to the strongest weapon in my mother's arsenal—guilt.

That Sunday night, as I drove back to my real life in the city, I thought to myself, *This had better pay off someday or I'm really screwed.*

5

Momma and Homos and Shrinks, Oh My!

Cries of "Happy New Year!" resounded throughout the gay club in which I sat among cross-dressers, leather-clad hotties, and homosexuals of all shapes and sizes. Kisses and hugs followed, along with plenty of music and dancing. My crowd knew how to party even at a time when we were still far from accepted by mainstream society. It was the start of not only a new year but also a new decade—the sixties—and I ushered it in by drinking, dancing, partying, drinking some more, and seeking out someone, anyone, to take home with me.

But as the new year began to unfold, I found myself thinking less about my nonexistent love life and more about my work. Every minute I spent amid the bland merchandise of Detroit Furniture inspired me that much more to build up my client base and get the hell out of there. Of course, with the dreaded family motel in White

Lake draining me of whatever extra money I made, this would be no easy task. If I was going to make it on my own, I needed to kick my part-time interior design business into high gear. To position myself better among high-class clientele, I decided to move on up from the Village and install myself in a chic Sutton Place apartment. Making this change not only allowed me to display my refined taste to clients firsthand, but also moved me closer to the D&D Building and gave me easier access to the varied antique shops in the area.

Nestled along the East River, Sutton Place was tucked away in an area zoned for quiet residential life. The pre-war apartment buildings and brownstones were designed to impress the gentry, and they succeeded in doing so. While it was farther away from my cherished gay life in the Village clubs, the new apartment provided a more impressive address for my business cards, which I handed out to people on every possible occasion. Besides, I was now a bit closer to the midtown movie houses of Broadway and all the anonymous sex they had to offer.

Slowly, the word spread about the room I had designed for Marguerite Piazza, the assistance I had provided with Ms. Streisand's apartment, and the decorating projects I had completed for wealthy clients. I worked quickly, and I worked for less. After a few jobs that came in at random, I began to win clients at a far steadier rate—just fast enough to keep pace with all those checks I was sending out to my parents. I was getting calls from the Upper West Side, Park Avenue, Sutton Place, and even Westport, Connecticut, all fashionable, well-to-do neighborhoods. I even designed the living room for a young singer from Astoria, Queens, born Anthony Benedetto, but known to the world as Tony Bennett. His decision to change his name for his career was not too different from my own decision to transform Eliyahu Teichberg into Elliot Tiber.

To my way of thinking, the cocktail party circuit was an important part of being connected with potential clients, and there were plenty of cocktail parties to attend. This was especially true whenever I finished a job. Often, satisfied customers would invite their affluent friends to their homes to see my work and to meet me, the snazzy decorator.

At one cocktail party, I met the then-popular performer Bea Kalmus. Bea had started out as a nightclub singer and later became New York's first female DJ. At that time, she hosted a radio show called *The Bea Kalmus Show,* which was broadcast from a Manhattan night spot. Bea invited me to be a guest on her show, and my absurdist humor was so well-received that I soon became a regular. Each week, I talked about decorating and whatever meshugas came to mind. The show attracted its share of celebrity listeners, and my interviews drew calls from Cyd Charisse, Tony Martin, Clayton Moore, and even Eydie Gormé along with her singer husband, Steve Lawrence. I was overwhelmed by the attention and encouragement of these stars, and they seemed delighted by my offbeat sense of humor.

Bea also went to endless parties. Perhaps she needed a boy toy at her side because she soon started to schlep me along with her, always with her dominating Jewish momma pulling up the rear and giving Bea instructions on what to say and how to say it. It was ridiculous how her mother went everywhere with her—to parties, to dinners, on shopping excursions, and even to her radio broadcasts. Bea's mother reminded me a lot of Momma, except that Mrs. Kalmus dressed much better. She didn't wear aprons wherever she went, and her high heels were actually *high* heels, as in a few inches off the ground. My Momma would never have worn such things for fear of falling.

Despite having her momma along, or perhaps because of it, Bea and I met dozens of celebrities wherever we went, and many of them wound up asking me to decorate their homes. What I quickly came to learn, however, was that these opportunities often came with a catch. Even though my fees were below market prices, many celebs wanted me to work for free. "Once people know you did our home, you will be swamped with show biz clients," I was often told. There was no way I could afford to donate my services, though, let alone the furnishings. These people obviously didn't know I had an albatross called White Lake around my neck.

Clearly, I would not remain long at Detroit Furniture. The owners loved me, but I hated the subway ride to Greenpoint, Brooklyn as well as the company's lackluster merchandise. The salary was the only thing that kept me coming back each morning—that is, until the Shapiros came into my life.

One afternoon, a couple wandered into the store. We started talking and it seemed that we had a lot in common. Lou and Erica Shapiro hated the furnishings as much as I did, but loved the room layouts, as well as the paintings that were hanging on the walls. When I let them know that I had designed the model rooms and that most of the paintings were mine, they explained that they needed someone to redecorate their home. They were certainly not interested in using anything they found in that store, however.

Fully aware of the many ways in which Plaza Interiors attracted business, I worked hard to dazzle the Shapiros with my wit and wisdom. I made it clear that my job at Detroit Furniture was just a steppingstone on the way to bigger and better things. I mentioned W. & J. Sloane, B. Altman's, and Marguerite Piazza. I even invited the couple to my apartment, where my growing treasure-trove of collectibles was quite a sight—even if much of it was far less valuable than it appeared to be. The Shapiros were impressed and asked me to dinner at their sprawling classic six (six-room) apartment on West End Avenue. They were right; the place truly needed a makeover. They had redecorated the apartment twenty-five years before, and it still smacked of their Bronx origins.

Lou Shapiro was a very successful furrier. His wife, Erica, was a genuinely open and sincere woman with a terrific sense of humor. They had two sons—one was married, and the other was a teenager living at home. Their youngest son joined us at dinner, so I was careful not to let my absurdist remarks wander too far afield. During the meal, I asked the Shapiros how they envisioned their apartment and carefully listened to what they had to say. I then freely offered some ideas for their consideration based on what I had seen of their home. As supper concluded, we agreed to make the rounds of New York's best showrooms the following day.

After a few days of schlepping around the city with Lou and Erica, I sketched all my concepts for the various rooms. I then returned to their apartment, drawings in hand. They liked what they saw and asked when I could begin. The three of us had been dancing around together for nearly a week, and it was now my turn to lead.

Since the beginning of Plaza Interiors, I had deliberately underpriced my services to stimulate interest and inquiries. Now I felt ready to charge the rates of a top Manhattan decorator. I really did not want to lose my clients over the fee, but it was time for me to make some real money. I smiled, held my breath, and presented them with my service contract. Lou didn't blink an eye. He read the agreement over, signed it, and never once quibbled about the price. Within a week, I would start on a fabulous job for fabulous pay.

Careful not to "quit my day job," I called in sick for a week as I decorated my butt off for this dream couple in their palatial apartment. I painted murals in their foyer and made their old piano look like a Versailles masterpiece. Because they loved small gardens, I designed a charming gazebo and filled it with artificial plants so that they could enjoy a garden without having to tend it. In short, I did my best to satisfy their every whim. In return, they not only paid me handsomely but also bought a few of my paintings.

When the apartment was complete, the Shapiros were ecstatic. They felt as if they were living in a *House Beautiful* magazine spread. I, too, felt wonderful because I had helped them create a living space they would enjoy for years to come. Better yet, Erica and Lou treated me as if I were their son and continued to invite me to dinner even after my work was done.

To celebrate their magnificent new home, Erica and Lou decided to throw a huge party for dozens of their friends and business associates. They chose a Friday night in July, a time when I would normally be making my Jekyll-to-Hyde transformation as I motored up to White Lake. I told Momma that I had a very important party to attend. She didn't understand, but before she could begin her rant, I quickly explained that the gathering was for the faculty of Hunter College. That was enough to make it acceptable to Momma. As long as I was making good as a professor, I could drive up on Saturday.

As a final treat for the Shapiros, I asked Marguerite Piazza if she would join me at the housewarming. Graciously, she agreed, which thrilled both my clients and their friends. I secured four jobs by attending that one housewarming. Instantly and joyfully, I bid farewell to Detroit Furniture and made Plaza Interiors my full-time business.

At last, I felt a sense of accomplishment. I had started a business with a single ad in *The New York Times* and was now commanding high fees as a decorator. Parties, openings, and all sorts of fashion events were on my calendar, and I was hobnobbing with the "in crowd." Rather than being a member of the performing arts community or a hairdresser, I was lucky enough to be an interior designer. In my field, it was both acceptable and très chic to be homosexual. After all, while they may not have realized it, none of my clients wanted to hire a straight decorator!

🌴 🌴 🌴

During these upwardly mobile years when my career was taking off, I still spent nearly every weekend of every spring and summer with my parents in White Lake. The drive up from the city was nearly three hours in traffic, and had me travelling from highways to local streets to the unpaved roads around the lake. The more deserted the road, the closer I was to our wretched White Lake motel.

Summer after summer, weekend after weekend, I did what I could to help my parents in their endless quest to attract guests. In 1961, in another attempt to spruce up the motel's shabby décor, I was able to obtain eight luxury sofas. In the course of my work as a decorator, I had befriended a woman named Beth Knipshultz, who ran a Danish modern sofa showroom. I liked the clean lines of her furnishings and often ordered them for my clients. One evening, Beth told me that a truckload of leather sofas was on its way from Toronto to the manufacturer due to product imperfections. In those days, such rejects were often dropped off at the Salvation Army, although in some cases, exhausted drivers would simply dump the furniture in empty lots in the Bronx, where they were scavenged by locals. Since this "reject sofa" truck would be passing through Sullivan County in upstate New York, I figured the drivers could deliver the sofas to the motel. Beth had visited the White Lake fiasco once on a dreary off-season weekend, so she knew the motel could use all the help it could get. Kindly, she agreed to divert the truck.

I called Momma and shared the good news. "But the office is only seven by nine feet, Eliyahu," she protested. "Those sofas are over seven feet wide! We hardly have room for a stool, let alone some fancy schmancy sofa!"

After telling Momma not to worry, I asked to speak to my father. "Pop, knock down a wall," I said. "We have a luxury sofa coming for the main office, plus a few more!" He understood and got right to work.

I thanked Beth and promised to give the drivers a free weekend at the motel during off-season. Of course, she knew that this was no bargain. "Once they see that dump, Elliot, they will race right out of your driveway," she said. "Better give them ten dollars in cash."

The truck arrived with the leather sofas, eight just for us. A few even had leather throw pillows. The drivers just dumped the furniture out on the front driveway. Good thing it wasn't raining. Dad broke open the wooden wall of the office and put up another plywood wall, thereby making the space large enough for an elegant Danish modern sofa. Two bungalows whose only seating consisted of nail barrels would now also have a lovely touch of Denmark. We managed to squeeze one into what I called the "Greta Garbo" wing of our motel, and another on the porch of the "Bette Davis" bungalow. I entertained the fantasy that *House Beautiful* magazine would hear about my imaginative decorating solutions and photograph them for an article called "Decorating With a Bupkis Budget." Well, maybe not. Nonetheless, our motel was now the crowded home of eight semi-fine sofas that were certain to please our guests—if only we had some. I knew that Pop truly appreciated my efforts but was too exhausted to say anything. Momma, of course, never appreciated anything I did. Nope, I was still her loser son who wasn't a rabbi and hadn't given her any grandchildren.

🌴 🌴 🌴

While the Danish modern couches did add some class to my parents' motel, the few tourists who drove by us on Route 17B did just that—they drove by and continued on their merry way. But I refused to give up. There had to be some way to turn our albatross into a cash cow.

The next summer, I had another brainstorm: Since booze was a foolproof way to make money, we would convert the coffee shop and lobby area into a bar! The only problem was that the town would not give us a liquor license. Undeterred, I pored over the recorded documents at Town Hall and found a loophole. As a motel, we couldn't serve liquor, but as a hotel, we could. *Hotel*, I thought, hmmm. . . . So I painted over the "M" in the motel sign with a big letter "H" and presto, we got the liquor license. Of course, Momma, Pop, and I weren't so easily fooled. We knew it would always be a motel.

To satisfy the rule that food had to be served by any establishment that offered liquor, we served Stuart's Infra-Ray Hot Sandwiches. Momma wouldn't handle the sandwiches because they were not kosher, but on the rare occasion that someone actually bought one, she would set aside her kosher principles just long enough to serve the sandwich and collect the cash.

My one saving grace in the endless White Lake nightmare was that I got to convert the barn into a small summer theater where I could perform my comedy monologues. I had always wanted to try my hand at stand-up comedy, and here was my opportunity. At my first performance, nobody showed up. Scratch that; Momma dropped in for a few minutes to watch me as I stood there talking, talking, talking to the empty air. I shared the old show-biz axiom, "The show must go on!" She demonstrated support for my creativity as only she could: "Yutz! I told you not to make a theater! Who needs a theater? And you, Mr. Comedian, you're not even funny. Nobody wants to hear your stories!" And with that, she ran back to the motel. *Pretty amazing,* I thought. *No audience and I still had a heckler.*

Pop was more encouraging. In a rare moment, he actually opened his mouth and spoke, saying that it would take time to get a new theater working. When July brought the tourists, he assured me, the seats would be full. At least he made an effort to be supportive.

Year after year, nothing changed. The motel made no money, and Momma failed to appreciate anything I did. No matter how successful I was in my decorating career, no matter how many celebrities I met at parties, I was miserable, because as soon as I returned to White Lake, I was again that insecure kid from Bensonhurst, trying in vain to please Momma. Some people try to recapture their youth . . . mine kept trying to recapture me.

🌴   🌴   🌴

White Lake was certainly a nightmare, but unfortunately, it wasn't the only troubled aspect of my life. Countless parties had introduced me to potential clients and even life-long friends, but had failed to give me what I wanted most—a real romantic relationship.

To relieve my sexual frustration, I spent seventy-five percent of my leisure time in the Times Square "grindhouse" movie theaters, which showed porno movies, Westerns, and old foreign flicks. But nobody came to see the films. The draw was the sexual activities in the theater itself, always anonymous and frequently dangerous. There was endless action in the seats, the dark corners of the lower level, and the recessed staircases. Even as a kid, I had found it exciting, and as an adult, I made out every time I went there.

While most of the guys I came in contact with were gay, the theaters also had their share of hustlers and muggers, and some men even had knives. Those were the ones I found most alluring. On a couple of occasions, I almost got slashed or stabbed, but quick thinking and even quicker feet saved me.

I also visited the piers, where supposedly straight sailors would often hook up at night with horny visitors like me. This sex, too, was anonymous, dangerous, and exciting. Even after moving uptown, I continued to make the rounds of movie theaters and downtown piers, since chic Sutton Place offered nothing comparable.

During much of the sixties, one of the most popular hangouts for gays in Manhattan was a former 1920s speakeasy called Lenny's Hideaway. Located on Seventh Avenue South, this basement nightclub was always packed, probably because there was little competition. Gay clubs were often shut down by the cops for breaking any number of the local anti-homosexual laws that were then on the books. This made the club scene risky in its own way; you never knew when the police would burst in and round everyone up. Cops had no problem roughing up "fags," and often hauled them off to holding cells for further humiliation. In addition, homophobic thugs enjoyed hanging out near the bars for the sole purpose of beating up patrons as they left for home. It was not unusual for the cops to turn the other way, since beating up "homos" was only a misdemeanor. For those of us who frequented the bars, it meant exiting swiftly and watching to see if we were being followed. I made it a habit to walk as directly as possible from the club to a taxi. Thankfully, that area always had several taxis cruising the main avenues, as they knew where the action was.

Although I did spend some time in bars and clubs, my self-image as a fat, ugly Jewish guy made it difficult for me to enjoy their competitive atmosphere. I preferred to look for Mr. Right at smaller parties. I also felt that private parties were safer than clubs; no police or homophobes were hanging around, waiting to harass and batter gay clients. Even when I no longer threw my own parties, I was invited to other people's gatherings. Still, I rarely went home with anyone. To me, it seemed that only "the beautiful people" ended the evening in happy pairings. Most of the other partygoers were content to merely get drunk. Since drinking didn't bring me any relief, that was no solution. I still hungered for love and cried myself to sleep more often than I care to remember.

🌴 🌴 🌴

In the fall of 1960, I had begun dealing with severe bouts of depression. My sister Goldie suggested therapy and directed me to a program at Columbia University. I applied and was accepted by a Dr. Sidney Malitz. His clinical response to my rants about being "a fat, ugly misfit homosexual" was always, "Take these, and see if they help." They didn't, and I soon stopped taking them.

Freudian therapy remained the most popular school of psychological treatment at that time. I went to a half-dozen different shrinks, searching for one who might tell me something truly helpful. Alas, all those Freudians said nothing—cigar or no cigar. They listened, maybe, and took notes. I began to think that once a week, they all got together to share a laugh and compare notes: "Hey, you saw that Elliot character, too, right? What a loser! What did he tell you?"

Even though I didn't seem to be benefitting from the sessions in any way, I went to one therapist for several years. I'd talk, he'd listen. At each session, I discussed my parents, why I felt Momma could never give me any support or love, and how I kept seeking it anyway, even as an adult. Nearly every time I posed a question, the doctor would respond with another question.

"Why do I keep trying to please Momma?" I asked.

"Why do you *think* you're trying to please her?" the doctor replied.

"I feel like I was never loved as a child, and still don't feel that anyone will love me until I get her love. Could that be it?"

"Perhaps. How do you feel about that?"

"I feel fat, ugly, and worthless and want to kill myself. Now what?"

"Well, our time is up, so let's talk about that next time."

I kept looking for validation from the shrink, for acceptance from my parents, and for love from someone, anyone, but it was just not to be. Finally, when my treatment bill reached a total of nearly four thousand dollars, I told this useless excuse for a therapist that I was not paying him and was never coming back. To this, he replied, "We'll talk about that next time."

There was no next time. And ironically, he never sent me a bill.

If there was anything that kept me from going completely over the edge, it was music. Whether I was painting a canvas, restoring an antique end table, or sketching a room layout, I would select some choice LPs, load them onto my record player, and then concentrate on what I needed to do. I had used this method of coping during my incarceration in my parents' home and found it just as necessary in Manhattan, especially as my parents' reliance on me for cash continued to deepen my black moods. Whether it was opera, classical, or pop, music softened the loneliness, lessened the pressures, and nurtured my creativity. Of course, my favorite popular songs were those sung by Miss Judy Garland. I could listen to her for hours—and I did. Even if I hadn't found Mr. Right, I could always count on Judy.

In 1961, I read that Judy Garland was going to perform at Carnegie Hall sometime in April. I left work early to walk over to the famed concert hall, but the ticket seller explained that the Garland tickets wouldn't be available for at least two weeks. After the first week, I dropped by the hall every single day to see when the tickets were going on sale. I hoped that with repeat visits, the woman behind the glass would remember me. To my disappointment, she never appeared to recognize me, and always answered my questions coolly without returning my smile.

The day before the tickets went on sale, I called in to let the boss know I would be late. The next morning, I arrived at the hall at about five o'clock only to discover that the line stretched down the block. I took my place at the end of the growing line and waited . . . and waited and waited. After what seemed like an eternity, the box office opened and, thankfully, the line began to move. Finally, I made it to the top of the line.

Smiling at the lady I had come to know over the weeks, I said, "One ticket, please . . . ma'am."

The woman looked at me and stiffly replied, "Just wait one moment." She disappeared to parts unknown.

She couldn't have run out of tickets already! I thought. Maybe those daily visits hadn't been such a good idea after all.

The woman quickly returned to her post, though, and told me the price of the ticket. I slid the money under the glass, and she handed me a small envelope. Without cracking a smile, she said, "Enjoy the show." As I opened the envelope and pulled out the ticket to see the location of the seat, I couldn't help but laugh. Orchestra, tenth row, dead center!

The concert was scheduled for Sunday, April 23, and was going to be Judy's only New York City performance that season. When the day arrived, I made sure to get to the hall early. Unfortunately, the doors didn't open until fifteen minutes or so before showtime. As I waited, the crush of bodies continued to grow. By the time I got to my seat, I noticed two things. First, an amazing number of celebrities had come to watch and listen, and second, a large number of audience members were quite obviously gay. It was one thing to see gay men at bars or parties, but to see them in such high numbers at one event was an over-the-rainbow experience indeed. Of course, Judy had been an idol to the gay community for years, so in spite of the homophobic laws of the city, the mostly hidden gay men of Manhattan were not going to miss this very special concert.

Judy was the only act that night and when she walked onto the stage, the audience went wild. The crowd's roar was louder than anything I'd ever heard before—louder even than Momma's screams. The concert lasted for over two hours, and if you asked anyone in the audience, they would have agreed that it could have gone on for at least another two hours. Judy was spectacular. She sang every song as if it were her last. When she performed "The Man That Got Away," I was so riveted by the raw loneliness and desperation in her voice that I didn't feel the tears stream down my face until the song had ended. And when she sang "Over the Rainbow," I was again that little boy in the Brooklyn movie theater—and here was my guardian angel, promising me bluer skies and happier days.

When Judy first left the stage that night, I was among the hundreds of people who got to their feet, wildly applauding and asking for more. We kept calling her back for encore after encore. At one point, the lovely lady said that she would sing to us all night if we wanted. "I don't ever want to go home," she said in words that seemed to be aimed directly at me. I knew exactly what she meant since no place I had lived had seemed like "home" in any true and meaningful sense.

That night, I left Carnegie Hall feeling utterly mesmerized, and for the next three months or so, I played only Judy Garland records. In July, when the double album of the concert was released, I listened to it over and over again.

The next time I was to see Judy perform live was in 1967, when she was headlining at Broadway's Palace Theatre. The show was booked for four weeks, and I was definitely not going to miss her. My income had increased significantly by then, as had my growing debt in White Lake. But I had also learned a lot since that 1961 concert. This time, instead of standing on line for hours, I was able to get a front row seat with just a phone call to a client who was a theatrical agent. When I arrived at the theater, at least ninety percent of the audience was composed of gay guys. By now, even the straight world knew that Judy was our leader and heroine.

I was in my seat early, holding a dozen white roses in my lap. When Judy made her appearance, I stood up quickly and presented the flowers to her. She blithely accepted my gift, and then—ever the gracious lady—handed one rose back to me. I kept it pressed in a book for many years. Judy did not disappoint; she was fabulous that night. And this time when she performed "Over the Rainbow," I felt that she was singing only to me. For a few minutes, I could see that I was someone special, someone with a better life over that rainbow—if I could only find it for more than one night. The all-too-short evenings I spent watching Judy Garland did far more for me than all those years of so-called therapy.

🌴　🌴　🌴

Perhaps I was inspired by Judy's latest concert, but soon after the show, I decided to move yet again. This time, I would find a new and even better place to call home. In fact, I decided to create my very own Land of Oz.

I wanted something really special, perhaps even a classic nine—a nine-room apartment. They were extremely hard to come by and very expensive. One of my ex-boyfriends, Allan, whom I had seen for a couple months back in 1962, had inherited his father's real estate business and become an overnight property maven. Despite our breakup, he still enjoyed my paintings. Backed by the force of his real estate empire, Allan hired me to paint murals in the lobby of a building on East Eightieth Street. Out of my paint tubes flowed faraway and exotic Rome with its Trevi Fountain, winged cherubs and bluebirds of happiness, and even a subtly rendered yellow brick road. With Judy as my muse, why not?

I told Allan that I was looking for a classic nine in a building with a doorman. He told me about one at 161 West Eighty-Sixth Street, just down the block from Central Park. The apartment had nine huge rooms occupying a good portion of the top floor. It was in a turn-of-the century building and included every amenity except a garage. Lack of parking, I told him, would not be a problem. He then said I'd need a couple of thousand dollars for key money. A common enough practice at the time, key money was essentially a bribe given to a landlord to secure a sought-after apartment. You paid the money in cash and it was kept off the books. Landlords loved it, of course, especially when high-end apartments provided high-end payments. In this case, I was just about to tell good ol' Allan where he could stick his key money when he made me an offer I couldn't refuse.

"Give me six Rothko-type oil paintings, and you can move in," he suggested, ready to foot the bill in exchange for my work. Allan was convinced that my art would someday be worth a fortune. In this case, it was worth a small fortune, as he billed his late father's company five thousand dollars per painting. He made out like a bandit, but I didn't care. I had found my dream apartment.

The rent was three hundred dollars a month at a time when most rentals cost sixty-five to eighty-five dollars. By this point, though, I was making terrific money and had a long list of wealthy clients waiting for me to redesign their homes. Of course, White Lake was continuing to drain me of significant amounts of cash, but I still generated enough income to make it all work. My accountant, Ira Levine, pointed out that if I dedicated several rooms to showing my antiques, paintings, and accessories, I could write off part of the rent as a business expense. Suffice it to say, Ira was a very good Jewish accountant.

I stood outside the twelve-story building and looked up in amazement. My work had taken me to many beautiful buildings, but this one was different. An imposing red brick structure designed in the Italian palazzo style, this was going to be my home. As I walked towards the entrance, the handsome uniformed doorman asked who I was there to see. I said, "I guess I'm here to see . . . me. I'm the new tenant in 12A."

"Welcome to the building. I'm Ralph. If you have any questions about the place, please ask."

"This is really a nice place," I replied.

"Yes, sir. It was built in 1915 and currently has fifty-eight separate apartments."

"Are there a lot of fancy people living here?"

"I don't know if they're fancy, sir, but they seem to be quite successful."

"Then I'm glad I could join the gang."

Two weeks later, I made the move. I was in heaven. For city dwellers, a classic nine is the top of the line. Designed for New York's well-to-do, my apartment boasted a forty-foot marble-floored entry hall that served as the common area. One set of doors led from this formal foyer to a spacious living room, which was adjacent to a music room. Another set of doors led to a formal dining room, and off the dining room was a library or smoking room. The rest of the living space, also accessed from the foyer, included the kitchen, the maid's room, and—separate from the rest of the apartment—three bedrooms, with the master suite tucked away in the back. Many of the rooms contained beautiful fireplaces. And, of course, there were bathrooms everywhere. The apartment had a southern exposure, which meant that it was filled with natural light throughout the day.

My classic nine became my new canvas. As a first step, I found a vintage jukebox, which I had installed in the music room. I filled the jukebox with Judy Garland records so no matter which button you punched, up popped Judy. I then covered the walls with murals that resembled the interior of New York's Palace Theatre.

Judy would now sing against a backdrop of red velvet seats filled with attentive fans.

I had stayed in touch with my decorator friend and early mentor Curtis Murray, and offered him bargain-basement prices for furniture that his clients had declined to purchase. The French *recamier*—a backless couch—had Louis XV gold-carved swan arms and legs, and was upholstered in a rich purple-and-silver brocade. It looked divine in front of the mahogany baroque mirror, which took up a full fifteen feet of wall space in the entry hall. I painted the walls a hysterical purple and installed several hot pink spotlights around the immense crystal chandelier, which dated back to my days at B. Altman's. The oriental rug looked completely authentic in such a splendid room. It was a steal from the Salvation Army.

The living room was all Persian gardens and featured a huge blowup photograph of the Taj Mahal. I dabbed paint on the photo to make it look like a work of art, figuring that my Upper West Side clients would never know the difference. At the time, I was designing a showroom for Fifth Avenue's Gift Building and had over-ordered faux topiaries and rhododendrons. A dozen of these plants found a home in my Persian garden. The fifty-foot expanse of wall needed the refined artistry of a Persian tapestry, but there was no way I could spend thousands of dollars for the real thing. My solution was to buy three copies at Village rug auctions for only a hundred dollars apiece.

I was on a roll, very excited about using the apartment for parties and as a selling space for clients. David, a friend who worked at a warehouse near Coney Island, had six small carousel horses that were just taking up space. He was more than happy to let me have them at fifteen dollars each, and even threw in a bunch of old neon signs that had been discarded by the amusement park. The question was, what to do with the horses? I called my favorite carpenter, whom I had met through Curtis, and he helped me level the legs of the brilliantly colored animals. He then fastened rubber and felt pads to their heads and topped the pads with a two-inch-thick glass tabletop. A little of this, a little of that, and I had a one-of-a-kind dining room table! This would help me welcome potential clients, not to mention the melting pot of new and old friends that I would invite to my digs.

Once the table had been completed, I again took out my mural brushes and paints. First, I recreated Steeplechase Park and Coney Island strictly from memory. Then, I hung the dozen neon and electric signs, which advertised a peep show, hot dogs, the laughing fat lady, and a devil with horns from a haunted house amusement ride. As I stood back to admire my own creations, I realized that something was missing. I wanted to stimulate senses other than sight and touch; I needed the crash of ocean waves. A friend who created sound effects for Broadway shows installed a sound machine behind a statue of Napoleon. True, the statue didn't fit my amusement-park theme, but with a sale price of less than four dollars, I hadn't been able to resist.

The buffet also had to be spectacular. Nothing run-of-the-mill would do. So I schlepped out to a Staten Island warehouse filled with abandoned Broadway set pieces that could be had for very little money. The instant I saw the table, I had to own it. A relic from a 1930s vampire play, it was at least twelve feet long and had hideous gargoyle legs. On its ornately carved top lay assorted medieval torture instruments. The warehouse guy let me have the table for seventy-five dollars cash and the torture items for nothing. Apparently, people didn't appreciate the decorative value of fine medieval tools. I used the table as a buffet and turned the instruments into a second chandelier by welding them together and adding a string of small lights.

My new kitchen was in need of dishes, and I wanted only the best. I knew that when restaurants and hotels went bankrupt or chose to upgrade, their old monogrammed tableware usually ended up at restaurant and hotel supply outlets, where it was sold for next to nothing. So I travelled down to the Bowery outlets. There, I was able to make selections from the Waldorf, the Plaza, the Carnegie Deli, the White House, and even several ocean liners and railroad dining cars. No, I didn't get a matching set, but my guests would never notice; they would be overwhelmed by the rest of my apartment.

I couldn't settle for Plain Jane bathrooms, either, as that would break the theatrical illusion I had created throughout the apartment. So I concocted my own Brazilian rain forest, a gypsy fortune-teller's tent, an ugly Grand Central train toilet with a coin slot door (I had a plate of coins handy, of course), and lastly, a Spanish Inquisition torture chamber. I couldn't find black toilet paper so I was forced to use white. Nobody complained.

My own bedroom was, of course, all black, including leather walls, black leather floor covering, and black leather sheets and bedspread. A huge photo of Judy Garland in a black leather frame stood as the centerpiece.

Among the first people to visit my fabulous new apartment was my accountant, Ira Levine. He was indeed the stereotypical accountant, with the quintessential suburban home, the gracious wife to greet him with supper every evening, and probably the standard two and a half kids. For Ira, touring my apartment was like visiting an amusement park that was dazzling, weird, and even scary. He loved the place. After the grand tour, we sat down for a drink. While he sipped red wine and I enjoyed an egg cream, Ira explained the realities of living in Disneyland.

Ira made it clear that I was just about solvent. I was getting by, in part, by writing off the losses incurred by my parents' motel. He went on to explain that if I wanted to continue my classic-nine lifestyle, I would need to either close down the place in White Lake or increase revenues from my interior design business. As much as I wanted to shut down the motel, I did not want Momma and Pop living with me. What a frightening thought that was!

My only option—my grand plan—was to use the new apartment to showcase my talents and bring in clients at top rates. The enchanted world just beyond the rainbow was plainly in sight.

6

The Judge and the Bar

The new apartment was ideal for throwing parties. It had plenty of room, a well-equipped kitchen where hired chefs could prepare eclectic cuisine, and a jukebox full of Judy. As had long been my habit, I encouraged invited guests to bring their friends along. This made the evenings far more exciting since I was sure to meet new people to whom I could give the grand tour—which was not only my favorite new pastime, but also a great way to display my skills as a decorator. My accountant had made it very clear that if I were to support both my own lifestyle and my family's struggling motel, I needed to build my decorating business. Parties allowed me to expand Plaza Interiors while having a great time.

At one of my parties, I noticed a young woman, drink in hand, perusing my paintings. She wore a black lace camisole and a hot pink miniskirt, and she looked familiar. As I approached, I realized that she was an old friend from Midwood High School, which both Renee and I had attended. Her name was Tanya, and she had frequently visited our home to hang out with Renee. She was hard to forget because, for reasons that to this day remain unknown, Tanya never wore shoes. This always amazed me because the sidewalk was littered with so much dog poop, not to mention broken glass and other debris. Why would she take a chance? As I introduced myself, I couldn't resist glancing down at her feet, and was more than a little disappointed to find she was wearing a pair of red Joan Crawford ankle-strap shoes.

Tanya and I hugged warmly and struck up a conversation. Renee had invited Tanya to see my new apartment, and she absolutely loved the theatrical over-the-edge décor. Apparently, Tanya was still somewhat of a free spirit. She said she dabbled in dance, among other things, but was very vague about what she did for a living. She did, however, mention an "acquaintance" of hers, Supreme Court Justice Marcus Susskind. She recalled that he was in need of a decorator to furnish the Long Island mansion he had bought for his wife, Rose. Tanya explained that Rose didn't want to live in the city and wasn't enjoying the 'burbs, either. I could certainly relate to the dilemma of volleying between two places and two ways of life. As it turned out, Rose preferred the old Bronx apartment in which they had spent their early years of marriage. At that time, her husband was a young lawyer who actually came home at night. Of course, I later found out that Tanya knew all these details because she was the reason the judge no longer spent his evenings with Rose.

With a well-proportioned dancer's body, Tanya had become a model and a "B" movie actress—and that was "B" for bad, although she had a certain grace and pluck that most of those movies lacked.

As luck would have it, the police had raided the warehouse "movie studio" where Tanya was shooting a scene for one of those low budget skin flicks, and had arrested everyone involved. Apparently, the movie was said to appeal only to prurient interests and therefore was in violation of New York's decency laws. During one of Tanya's resulting courthouse appointments, she bumped into his honor in the hallway. Since modeling and acting weren't paying the bills—especially after the police ended her latest shoot—Tanya became a highly paid call girl.

Tanya said that she was still pursuing an acting career and asked if I knew anyone in the business. I told her I would ask around for her and applauded her determination. I also thanked her for the lead to a potential client. The conversation ended quickly, however, when she rushed out a breathless "Nice talking to you" while making a beeline for some tall Rock Hudson type standing at the opposite end of the living room.

I called the judge the very next day. I explained that a mutual friend of ours had suggested that I contact him regarding his need for an interior decorator. Oddly, he never asked about the mutual friend, but he was more than agreeable when I suggested that we get together near the downtown courthouse.

At our meeting the next afternoon, I found that the judge was a pleasant-looking man in his sixties—the image of a good husband, a sweet and caring grandfather. He was kind and had a superb sense of humor. We hit it off instantly.

I began by giving the judge my shpiel about my background and the various homes that I had decorated. More than anything, he wanted me to make his wife, Rose, happy by decorating their— *her*—Long Island home. He also uttered four words that I always loved to hear: "Money is no object." But before anything could be decided, I had to meet Rose. He warned me that she had very high standards and was difficult to please. Of course, he left out the part about her being a bit unwired.

The judge's limo arrived at ten in the morning to take me to his mansion in Muttontown, an exclusive area on the north shore of Long Island. After an hour-long drive, the limo turned onto an impressive circular driveway surrounded by well-tended lawns complete with statues, beautiful flower beds, and a working fountain. Obviously, the landscaper had great taste. The limo came to a stop in front of the stone steps leading up to the front door. As I climbed out of the car, I glanced up at the two massive entry doors. They were not matched. The one on the left had five rows of small window panes, reminiscent of a Frank Lloyd Wright design. The other door was Medieval Gothic—something you'd see at the entrance of a European castle. As I used the iron knocker on the right-hand door, I thought, *This is going to be interesting.*

A uniformed maid answered the door and ushered me in. "Mr. Tiber," she said, "The judge and Mrs. Susskind are waiting for you in the dining room. Please come this way, and be careful not to trip over the piles of carpet samples."

As the polite young woman and I crossed the foyer, I couldn't help but notice the truly strange décor. But I had little time for observation, as we soon entered the dining room. There, the judge was seated at the head of a large parsons table. As I entered, he stood up and smiled. The woman seated opposite from him, however, did not even look up at me, but stared impassively at the china coffee cup in front of her.

"Elliot, so glad you could make it," the judge said. "This is my wife, Rose. Honey, this is Elliot Tiber, the interior designer I wanted you to meet. I think he can help us decorate our home."

After shaking the judge's hand, I turned to his wife. "Good morning, Mrs. Susskind. The judge told me that you could use a little help finishing up some of the projects in your lovely home. I think I can be of some assistance."

Slowly, Mrs. Susskind turned her head to look at me and said in a quiet voice, "Good." While the judge was impeccably dressed in a dark custom-made suit, his wife wore a faded pink chenille robe. Her hair was up in curlers and she wore no makeup. Here was the woman who, according to Tanya, wanted to return to the Bronx. Apparently, she was ready to do so in an instant.

As I extended my hand toward that of my new client, she stood up, revealing that if she had ever cared about her weight, she had stopped worrying about it years before. I took hold of her hand and tried to reassure her. "I will do everything I can to give you what you want," I said.

Mrs. Susskind turned her gaze downward to the hardwood floor. "I doubt it, but that would be nice," she said softly. At that moment, I knew this was not going to be easy.

As a designer, I had learned that it's important to get the client involved in the process from the very start. With this in mind, I made a suggestion. "Why not show me through your house? Tell me what you've already done and what you would like to accomplish."

Looking unsure, Mrs. Susskind turned to the judge for guidance. The judge simply responded, "Please, Rose." She took a deep breath and directed me to follow her.

I had already walked through the entry hall, but it was only now that I fully appreciated its size. It was huge—perhaps two hundred feet in length—and was covered with a succession of different wallpapers, from watered silk to bamboo, from a delicate French toile to a bold stripe. There were a dozen different chandeliers, as well, ranging from ornate Rococo to sleek Danish modern. There were also six interior doors, each of which was of a different style. A traditional six-panel maple door stood a few yards away from a two-panel knotty pine. One door was a fine example of the prairie style of architecture, while another was richly carved with a Moroccan motif. Essentially, the house resembled a massive showroom; no cohesive theme could be found.

At first, Rose remained wordless and strangely detached as I examined the wallpapers, the doors, and the other elements that made up the massive foyer. Then suddenly, she began to speak.

"I know that we have a lot of different wall coverings and unmatched chandeliers," she said. "I couldn't decide which style I liked, so I decided to have them all installed so I could make up my mind."

Trying to be as helpful as possible, I asked if she preferred one design or material over the others.

Looking alarmed, she spoke more quickly, almost hysterically. "I wanted my husband to tell me which one *he* likes—which one *he* wants," she said. "But he's hardly ever home and when he is, he won't help me. Maybe *you* can find out what he likes."

I began to explain that the judge wanted most of all to create a home that would please his wife, but the floodgates had opened and Rose quickly interrupted. "I wanted at least a half-dozen children, but the judge never had time for that. He never had time for me. I made sure that *The Joy of Sex* was on the night table. He just wasn't interested!"

Rose appeared to be on the verge of a nervous breakdown. Trying to defuse the situation, I said that the judge had many professional responsibilities and probably spent many hours in the courtroom and chambers. Almost immediately, I realized that my choice of words had been poor.

"Chambers!" Rose cried. "Yes, but *whose* chambers? Probably some floozy or tramp. He keeps telling me that his court sessions often run until two in the morning, but whenever I call his office, his secretary says that she is not permitted to give out the location of trials. Probably even she doesn't know where he is!"

As the tour continued, Rose again lapsed into silence. Most of the rooms—all decorated with mismatched furnishings, just like the entry hall—were viewed without a comment. When it finally came time for me to leave, Rose could barely manage a whispered "Good-bye." I breathed a sigh of relief as I walked out the double doors.

The judge decided to accompany me on the ride back to the city. The limo had just turned off the driveway when the judge urgently explained that he needed his wife to be far away from the city. I could certainly see why. But did I really want to spend my days babysitting the judge's deeply unhappy wife?

🌴 🌴 🌴

Back in the city, I accompanied the judge to his chambers. "Before you say you don't want the job, you should know that I will pay you by the day since you won't be earning any commissions on furniture since Rose returns everything she orders," he explained. "I've made arrangements with all the decorator showrooms. I don't care how long it takes. And you can have use of my driver and car. The main thing is to keep Rose busy—busy and out of my hair."

I had mentally rehearsed my little speech several times on the way back from the Island, so I knew exactly what I was going to say.

"Your honor, it's not that I don't sympathize with your situation, it's simply that I already have enough difficult women in my life and if . . ."

"Elliot," the judge broke in, "I'll pay you two hundred dollars a day in cash. If you have to work on weekends, I'll pay you for that as well."

Two hundred dollars a day. Really, how much trouble could one woman be? "I'd love to take on the challenge," I said.

While I didn't know how much a judge was paid, I thought I'd discovered why the judge was staying in a marriage that had obviously fallen apart several years earlier. Perhaps Rose's family was supplying a sizeable trust fund. However he was getting the money, I was willing to do what was necessary to keep her out of his hair. Whether the situation called for creative design or babysitting, I was ready.

This is how my life became dedicated to shopping with Rose. We went from showroom to showroom and were treated well everywhere we went. The judge was obviously quite prominent and well-respected. That first month, we bought a half-dozen sofas. The showroom sent them to the house, and at Rose's orders, they were returned. Same thing happened with the bedroom sets—sent and returned—as well as tons of matching linens and accessories. Yes, I was making some very nice money, but Rose was driving me crazy with her hot-and-cold-running moods and her inability to stick with any decision. Then it dawned on me: Nothing pleased her because none of it meant anything to her. She was just filling in time and space. Whereas most of my clients felt joy when they saw the final results, none of the finished rooms gave Rose any pleasure. I needed to find something that would connect her to what we were doing. I had an idea.

"Rose," I said, "what are some of your favorite films?"

Rose said she hadn't gone to a movie for a while, but in years past, she had loved *Citizen Kane, Some Like It Hot,* and *Gigi,* among others. I suggested that we pick a room design from each of her favorite films—a turn-of-the-century French *Gigi* bedroom, for instance.

"Can we do that?" she asked in astonishment.

"We can do anything we want," I assured her.

"Let's start!" she said, laughing in delight.

Two months later, we had completed the *Some Like It Hot* entryway, the *Citizen Kane* dining room, and the *My Fair Lady* library. We had even installed *Adventures of Robin Hood* front doors. Rose had stopped sending things back and seemed to truly enjoy watching her home's interior take shape.

One evening, as I was sitting at home sketching out plans for the *To Have and Have Not* bedroom, I received a call from the judge. He explained that the situation with his wife had changed; she needed medical care. For the time being, my assignment was at an end. I told him how sorry I was—and I was—and wished both of them well. Working with Rose had almost become a full-time job, so I was somewhat relieved that I could again work on a variety of projects. Still, I had enjoyed the months I'd spent designing movie-themed rooms, and I had begun to understand the depth of her loneliness. Just as I was about to say good night to the judge, he told me that he had a very good friend who was in need of a decorator.

🌴　🌴　🌴

In the mid-1960s, New York City's social life was in full swing and offered something for practically everyone. From the Mine Shaft to the Peppermint Lounge to the Stork Club, it was all there—places to greet old friends, meet new people, dance till you dropped, be entertained, or just nurse a drink. There were so many night spots, in fact, that it was impossible to know them all.

I had heard of the Crystal Room but had never actually seen it. Located on the East Side on Fifty-Third Street, not far from Sutton Place, it had been around since the fifties. Its bar attracted a conservative older crowd, and its restaurant seemed to be filled with regulars. Like most clubs, it offered live musical entertainment. The owner—a friend of the judge—was Charley Gross, a former director of the New York Department of Public Works. Charley was in his mid-sixties and was strictly a no-nonsense type of guy. He knew that his club needed to be redone, and the judge had said that I was just the man to do it. That was enough for Charley, who hired me at the end of our first meeting.

Charley actually needed both his club and his penthouse redecorated, but wanted me to start with the nightclub. This made sense as the club's interior was dreary, grimy, and somewhat tacky. Almost every wall was covered with a dark maroon velveteen wallpaper and framed with dark wood molding, all of which appeared to be dusty and worn. Tiny spotlights made it all too obvious that the Crystal Room's flower arrangements were plastic and none too clean. I knew that I could spruce the place up while achieving the dignified elegance that the owner was seeking. After getting Charley's approval, I set things in motion.

First, I had the walls stripped clean and painted in warm deep reds. Along the walls, I added several of my own paintings—floral abstracts and New York City landscapes. The new replacement bar was a beautiful mahogany relic from a turn-of-the-century Bowery restaurant. All it needed was to be sanded smooth, stained, and polished. Once that was done, I spread the word that it was a copy of the bar in Al Capone's favorite speakeasy and had originally been installed in George Raft's Hollywood home.

While the Crystal Room's décor had definitely become outdated over the years, the good food had always drawn people in. So part of my arrangement with Charley was that I could get immediate seating should I bring any of my clients there for a fabulous steak or lobster dinner and show. The club provided entertainment in the form of a guitar-playing singer who went on to some recording success, and a show tunes pianist who accompanied aspiring female vocalists. Young, buxom, and beautiful, the singers had scant talent, but did bring in a steady stream of clientele who, while a little rough around the edges, spent their money freely on food and booze.

Charley explained that he had a strictly cash business, and would therefore be paying me in cash. I had no problem with that, since my parents also had a strictly cash business. The difference, of course, was that the Crystal Room was actually bringing in money. Being somewhat naive, I did ask the judge why Charley paid everyone in cash. The judge assured me that this was standard practice in the restaurant industry and was good business everywhere. Hadn't he paid me in cash? I quickly dropped the subject, not wanting to step on anyone's toes, especially my own.

Charley spent most of his time with Terry, a charming, sensitive woman of about fifty. Terry was exceptionally good-looking, reminiscent of the 1940s film star Joan Blondell. She was always smiling, at least around me, and was gracious to the customers, as well. She never spoke about her life before Charley and the Crystal Room, nor about family or friends. It was as if she had been born when she met Charley. Of course she had arguments with him in the dark recesses of the club, but I never knew what they were about. With me, she stuck mostly to the subjects of decorating, the club's food, and the club's entertainment. While I was fairly sure she knew I was gay, it was never mentioned.

I often had my meals with Terry, feasting on the club's ultra-expensive fare. I loved the steaks, the huge shrimp salads, and, of course, the endless bottles of champagne. Terry was much better company and infinitely more interesting then Rose. She was also kind and often told Crystal Room customers about my paintings and my talents as a decorator. I was happy to spend my time in the club. Why not? I was being paid to decorate, eat, and enjoy myself. I was sitting pretty, and I knew it.

Terry introduced me to many of the club regulars, who included several celebrities and other colorful characters. One of the most intriguing people I met was a gentleman named Mr. Joseph Marino. Marino was perfectly groomed and dressed in expensive suits—a little flashy, perhaps, but costly. A corner table was permanently reserved for him and his business associates, and the moment he entered the club, waiters ran to bring him his favorite cocktail, to make sure that he had everything he needed. Marino responded by giving the staff outrageously large tips.

It seemed a little strange that in a crowd of well-to-do and often high-profile people, it was Marino who seemed to receive the most attention. I also didn't know what to make of his associates, who sometimes appeared to carry guns under their jackets. When I mentioned this to Angelo, the bartender, he said the guys were probably bodyguards. Marino owned pieces of businesses all over the city, and like many powerful men, he needed protection whenever he was out in public. Angelo's explanation certainly sounded right to me.

🌴　🌴　🌴

Perhaps my favorite aspect of the Crystal Room was Tony, the tall, very handsome maitre d' with a wonderful Italian accent. He was always courteous and attentive, but for several months, our relationship was limited to superficial conversation. Then one night, after I'd treated a group of clients to a steak dinner, Tony slipped a piece of paper into my coat pocket and winked. The next night, he was in my apartment. Tony explained that neither Charley nor anyone else at the club knew—or ever *could* know—that he was gay. "Some of the regulars don't like 'fags,' " Tony explained, and his weary voice told me that he had probably heard that particular derogatory term far more often than he'd want to admit. "You don't want to piss them off," he added.

Within a very short period of time, my relationship with Tony blossomed. It was like a game. When I saw him at the club, we barely acknowledged each other beyond a polite greeting. We were sure never to leave at the same time, and always arranged to meet back at my apartment. For me, a two-month relationship was a lifetime, since almost all of my sexual adventures were one- or two-night stands.

Tony and I had been getting along extremely well when, suddenly and unexpectedly, everything changed. When I entered the club one night, there was a new maitre d'. I asked Terry if Tony was ill. Terry's face reddened as she whispered, "Tony was messing around with Mr. Marino's nephew, and Charley didn't want any trouble with those people. With you, it's different. You're an interior decorator. Also, the judge thinks the world of you. What you did with his wife and all."

I didn't quite know what Terry was talking about beyond the fact that Marino, an important patron of the Crystal Room, didn't like Tony's relationship with his nephew, so Tony had been fired. While I was upset about the possibility that Tony was having an affair during our time together, I tried reaching him later that night. No one picked up. I went to his apartment and knocked on the door. No one answered. I continued to call his number for weeks until a recording said that the phone was no longer in service. It all seemed very strange, and I was upset that my first relationship in some time had ended so abruptly.

As the weeks passed, feelings of loneliness once again engulfed me, but there was little I could do. I told myself that the relationship hadn't ended because of me, but because of Charley and his crowd's homophobia. Homophobia was something I understood. I knew never to let my personal lifestyle intrude upon my work at the club, so my decorating job seemed secure. But more nights than not, my jukebox was set to play Judy's recording of "The Man That Got Away." And again, my heart filled with sadness.

🌴 🌴 🌴

As sorry as I was to have Tony disappear from my life, I knew that I needed to concentrate on the task at hand, which was to decorate the club. From what I could see, that seemed to be progressing beautifully. Charley had little to say about my choices of colors, fabrics, paintings, or furniture, and since Charley generally spoke to employees only when there was a problem, I knew I was doing well. Although Terry was quite complimentary about my work, she often reminded me of how vital it was to please Charley and the judge. I assumed she meant that if they were satisfied with the job,

I would garner more work through their many contacts. After all, I had seen celebrities, prominent businessmen, and government officials spend time at the club. Why shouldn't I be the one who decorated their offices and homes at top-dollar prices?

Next up for me would be Charley's penthouse apartment—or so I thought. As the job at the club was winding down, Terry informed me that Charley's fiftieth birthday was coming up, and he had decided to throw himself a huge party. Instead of decorating his home, I would be arranging this mega-event with its "who's who" of celebrity guests, including none other than John Lindsay, the Mayor of New York City. This was a decorator's dream. Besides allowing me to hobnob with the city's elite, the event would surely attract an avalanche of press. This would be a marvelous opportunity, not only to do something outstanding for Charley, who had treated me so well, but to potentially break into the big time. It was one thing to be a busy designer and quite another to be one of Manhattan's "in" designers. I could charge ridiculous prices and still line up enough wealthy clients for a lifetime. My mind was swimming with the possibilities.

According to Terry, the party would be held on one of the Hudson River dayliners. Charley's guests would include political bigwigs, real estate magnates, Wall Street wizards, and theater people. The list of celebrities was impressive but held no real interest for me until Terry uttered the last name—a name that was as familiar and dear to me as any on earth. Attending the party would be Miss Judy Garland. After that, Terry could have saved her breath because her words had become indistinct and incomprehensible. All I could hear was the beating of my heart.

7

Somewhere Over the Hudson

I placed all my projects on hold. The fiftieth birthday party for New York City's former director of the Department of Public Works, Charley Gross, owner of the Crystal Room nightclub, was now my one and only job. Terry said that I was to create an upscale New York-style event. She put together a list of suppliers with which Charley had connections and explained that as long as I mentioned his name, they would extend all the credit I required. The list included companies that rented catering supplies, tables and chairs, theatrical props, and even high-fashion models—just about anything I might need to make magic—as well as a selection of local caterers. My budget would be twenty thousand dollars, and Charley would pay me after the affair.

The party was to take place on the *S.S. Peter Stuyvesant,* an old steam-powered dayliner that had long been used to transport tourists up and down the Hudson River. Like many other excursion vessels that plied the waters around Manhattan, the *Stuyvesant* had three spacious decks capable of holding over two thousand passengers. The first deck ran the full length of the boat—from the front of the ship to the back. This was the first area that arriving passengers would enter. The second deck sat atop the roof of the first deck. While mostly enclosed, it was surrounded by a wide exposed walkway that allowed passengers to stroll completely around the cabin. Above that was a once stately upper deck. In need of some repair, this deck was only partially enclosed and best suited for open-air dance parties.

For the most part, the *Stuyvesant* was geared for daytime excursions and holiday celebrations only. On this one night, though, the ship would be all mine to turn into a floating gala. There would be approximately five hundred guests, including New York socialites, Charley's intimidating business associates, and assorted club regulars. Both New York City Mayor John Lindsay and, most significantly for me, Judy Garland had been asked to attend. I would invite a gaggle of my own gay show-biz friends, assuming they would "blend in." They would *love* the chance to see Judy, and I would love giving them this opportunity. Hopefully, Charley would be too busy to notice the gay contingent.

I knew I had a short time in which to dream up a concept for the party. The theme should be exotic—something very different from the guests' everyday urban reality. After discarding a number of ideas, it came to me: The ship would transport its passengers to the Arabian Nights. Charley was a sultan in his own right, so I'd create a sultan's palace. Classical columns would add a sense of grace, a few dozen muscle boy guards would add a sense of fun, and palm trees would infuse the party with color and give guests an instant vacation from city life. I wasn't sure if the columns and palms truly fit the Arabian theme, but they would look great. And did I mention the muscle boys? I thought they'd look great, too. For good measure, I would add some harem girls for Charley's benefit. Strolling musicians also seemed to suit the Arabian Nights theme—at least, according to the countless "B" movies I'd seen. Zabar's, New York's crème de la crème of caterers, would handle the feast. This affair would treat guests to only the finest food that New York had to offer. No dried-out appetizers, rubbery chicken dishes, or watered-down cocktails on the *Peter Stuyvesant*!

As I jotted down notes on the event, more ideas came to mind. I would conjure up a gypsy fortuneteller and instruct her to give only thoroughly inventive readings. None of that "You're going to meet a tall dark stranger" mediocrity would do. It would be easy enough to find an attractive out-of-work actress, since most of them were waiting tables in the city's restaurants. And with the right attire and enough skin showing, she would delight Charley and his cohorts no matter what she said.

I wanted to make this a truly memorable occasion—a "happening" that even the most jaded of partygoers would find wildly entertaining. Maybe I'd hire four ponies for a real merry-go-round. Then I realized that where there's ponies, there's poop. Scratch the ponies. Instead, I could rent some carnival game booths and have them scattered around the boat in different locations. Maybe an ice skating rink would be a nice touch, but when I spoke to the captain, he made it clear that such a rink would not happen. Scratch the ice skating, too.

I visited one of the premier cake designers in New York City, Madame Svilenska Wallowich, and requested a very special birthday cake. In addition to serving five hundred guests, this custom-made confection would have a hollow interior so that a lovely blond girl who bore something of a resemblance to Marilyn Monroe could pop out as guests sang "Happy Birthday!" Of course, the cake would be the richest of devil's food covered with chocolate whipped cream—no bland and boring vanilla. Madame Wallowich determined the exact size of each portion scientifically. She then calculated the dimensions of what would be a masterful cake. I would have had more confidence in her calculations if I hadn't seen her snort some unidentified white powder. Nevertheless, she was on Terry's "recommended" list, so I assumed that she could do the job.

Of course, the guests would need somewhere to sit and enjoy their cake. The *S.S. Peter Stuyvesant* had a fair supply of old rickety wooden chairs and timeworn benches, but I knew that they didn't belong at my event. I would have them taken off the boat and replaced with hundreds of elaborately carved gold chairs with red velvet-covered seats. A stunning ice sculpture of Charley himself would be mounted on a lavish gold table—or, at least, on a table covered with a gold tablecloth. Throughout the planning process, I had to keep repeating to myself, *Stay within budget, stay within budget.*

The last order of business would be the look of the guards. I would have the scantily clad muscle boys covered in gold body paint to coordinate with the gold throne chairs that would be provided for Charley, Terry, the mayor, and Miss Garland. I would inspect each boy to make sure he had enough unpainted flesh to prevent skin suffocation. Fortunately, I had seen the James Bond flick *Goldfinger*, so I knew that a fully-painted body could be deadly. Filled with fantasies about meeting Judy, I imagined the gold-covered boys carrying her to a throne—it was just a thought.

Perhaps they could simply carry me around for a while—that was another thought.

I spent my days running from one supplier to another, and my nights figuring out how I would have it all ready on time. I wanted this to be my crowning achievement, not to mention a party that would be featured in all of the gossip columns. Just as important, I wanted to impress Judy. After all, she had been there for me whenever I needed her. Nothing would make me happier than creating a memorable evening for this wonderful woman.

🌴　🌴　🌴

The guests were scheduled to arrive at eight o'clock that evening. The boat would leave the pier an hour later, at nine. If any VIPs missed the boat, a small skiff would be available to transport them to the *Stuyvesant*. I had arrived at five in the morning with a small army of installers. There was a lot to be done, and I wanted to make sure that everything was set up properly and securely. I had drawn up plans that explained where each item should go and how it should look when it was in place. No ballet had ever been more carefully and lovingly choreographed.

The first-level entry deck would initially hold all the arriving passengers. Guests would be able to order drinks at several bar stations, while a small team of waiters would walk around with trays of pink champagne in fancy crystal glasses. This deck would also accommodate all the carnival games that I had rented.

Food and drink stations would be located strategically in each of the four corners of the second deck. Tables and chairs would allow the guests to sit once they had served themselves, while the long dais would be located near the back of the boat, but still close to the food. The nine-man band would be positioned on the second deck near the front of the boat. This would place the musicians at a comfortable distance from the dais. But everyone would be able to hear the music no matter where they were because we would set up speakers on all three levels of the ship. Additional bars would be arranged on the upper deck, which would be decorated with dozens of glorious rented palms. Now, I just needed everyone to follow my careful plan.

I had taped color-coded X's on the deck floors to indicate where everything was to be placed. A little after dawn, when the trucks arrived with the rental furniture, my staff knew that blue tape indicated the position of the large circular tables and chairs, red was for the bar stations, and green was for the buffet tables.

As each dining table was set in place, I had two teams of men standing by. One team double-draped each table with linen; the second, set the tables. Linen colors were alternated to provide greater drama. Some tables were covered first with white linen, then with black. The remaining tables were clothed first in white, then in gold lamé. Once the cloths were in place, glasses, silverware, and linen napkins followed—gold napkins on the black linen, and black on the gold. The same teams that set the tables would replace the guests' dirty plates and silverware throughout the event. The men moved quietly, gracefully, and calmly as they finished the table settings, arranged the buffet heaters, and readied the bar stations. Hand-picked, the staff was not only efficient but also very cute.

Now that the tables, buffets, and bars were in place, I turned my attention to the palm trees. I think I had rented every fake palm tree in New York City—three dozen in all. There were tall ones and short ones; some with large hanging fronds, others with small leaves. The bases on which they stood also varied. Some were narrow but weighted to prevent the tree from toppling over; most were wide to provide the greatest stability possible. I supervised the palms' placement as men from the rental companies carefully wheeled them onto the ship using hand carts. A few of the trees were arranged on the main deck, but the majority were positioned on the upper deck near the railings, providing a perfect visual counterpoint to the imposing Manhattan skyline.

I looked at my to-do list, and nearly everything had been done. The electricians had set up the band's microphones along with a public address system installed at the head table. The game booths were being put together. Tables? Check. Lights? Check. Palms? Check. The birthday sign for Charley? Not there. I called the company and was told that the truck carrying the sign had left more than an hour before. Alas, the enormous "Happy Birthday, Charley!" sign was stuck in traffic, and I had no way of reaching the driver. It was now seven. All the gold-painted guards were in position. The gypsy fortunetellers, the cake, and the Marilyn Monroe look-alike who was going to hop out of the cake—everything was ready to go, but we still had no birthday sign for the man who was footing the bill for this party. Twenty minutes before Charley and Terry were to arrive, the truck carrying the sign pulled onto the pier. We hustled to suspend the sign over the dais. The ice sculpture of Charley, already in place on the buffet, had a kind of Pinocchio nose—smooth but a little too long. *Oh, well, too late to change that,* I thought.

Finally, everything stood ready for the guests. The dining area looked like a five-star restaurant, the palm trees looked marvelous, and my golden muscle boys were simply divine. As I examined every inch of the ship, I was pleased. I had transformed an old-time

Manhattan dayliner into a floating palace fit for royalty—New York royalty included. Now, it was show time.

It was a warm night and there was no rain in the forecast. This was good, since there were no contingency plans for bad weather. After all, I was used to interior decorating; this was my first experience dressing up a boat. The limos began pulling up to the pier entrance, and from one of the longer vehicles stepped Charley with a group of friends, who looked more like a security team than the twilight revelers I had envisioned. Terry was beautiful. She wore an elegant black gown with many layers, cleverly hiding her decidedly Rubenesque figure, while Charley sported a sharp black tux. The couple gazed up at the formerly humdrum cruise ship to see my floating Arabian theme park, complete with a phalanx of gilded guards. They turned to each other and smiled. *They like it,* I thought.

I had invited Tanya, since it was her introduction to the judge and his introduction to Charley that had led to this once-in-a-lifetime event. She showed up with Renee, who wore what could have passed for a graduation gown now dyed electric blue. Tanya's ensemble made her look like a cross between a porn star and Ethel Merman—very low-cut and very loud, but lots of fun. The two friends could see I was exhausted and asked if there was anything they could do. I jumped at their offer and put them to work adding some last-minute touches.

The band assembled at the front of the ship so that any guests viewing the musicians would also see the water and the night sky. Once the sound equipment was up and running, the musicians began to warm up. There were half a dozen blowup pictures of Charley in place, and the party lights glowed in the dimming light. The caterers had done a superb job of displaying the food, which included shrimp platters, cheese and deli platters, and, of course, tons of bagels, lox, and cream cheese. Bar stations were ready to serve a hard-drinking crowd.

Limos brought some of the guests, others showed up in taxis, and a few—mostly, my Village crowd—made their way from the bus stop. Guests were now arriving at a steady pace, and the two harem girls who were collecting invitations had to work hard to avoid falling behind. At Charley's request, the media had not been invited to this floating party. Photographers were kept at a distance. As insurance, a few of Charley's extra-large associates, dressed in off-the-rack sharkskin suits, stood by the boat's gangplank to make sure that no flashbulbs popped and no reporters thrust their microphones into guests' faces. Charley and Terry seemed to value both their own privacy and that of their high-profile friends.

Charley and Terry greeted the party guests as they continued to come aboard. I was so busy with logistics that I didn't have time to size up who was who. Of course, I rushed to the front of the welcoming line once Mayor Lindsay arrived. Terry introduced me, and Charley told the mayor that I was the young man who had decorated the ship. Some minutes later, the judge arrived—without Rose. Instead, he escorted a bubbly young redhead with huge boobs that were nearly bobbing out of her elegant, backless—and nearly frontless—red satin gown.

I was working with my gold-painted boys, giving them instructions, when there was a huge outcry. Judy Garland had stepped out of her limo and was on the pier, approaching the ship. Several of the guests and many of my hired helpers rushed to the side of the boat to see her. As was her custom by this time in her career, she was accompanied by a small entourage. She was a shimmering vision in her sparkling black gown and gold jacket, but as she came closer, I could see that she looked tired. Fatigue aside, when she saw smiling fans calling her name and waving, she instantly sprang to happy, bouncy life with a broad smile appearing on her face. She was now "on." It seemed that yet another show was about to begin in the life of Miss Garland.

The crowd quickly settled down, and the golden boys moved back to their assigned positions. I tactfully but insistently placed myself at the head of the receiving line. As Judy came aboard, I introduced myself as the party planner and then introduced her to Charley and Terry, as well as a number of other VIPs. I then led her to her throne behind the dais on the main deck, and arranged for an unending supply of drinks. While she was not the guest of honor, it was clear that she was going to be the focus of everyone's attention.

Once Judy had taken her place, Terry rushed through the crowd and reminded me that it was time for Charley to be introduced. After all, nobody was going to upstage Charley on his special night—or so Terry thought. That evening, Charley was in an unusually jovial mood. He must have started drinking in the limousine on the way over, or at his club throughout the afternoon, or maybe just after breakfast. The birthday boy could normally hold his liquor, but by this point, the liquor may have gotten the best of him.

I walked over to the bandleader, a young Lawrence Welk clone in a painfully tight tuxedo, and handed him a list of the names that he would announce. He must have done this dozens of times because he looked quickly at the names, told the musicians what numbers they would play, and, without missing a beat, began speaking into the microphone. The dais was now full except for Charley, who waited out of sight.

"Ladies, gentlemen, and stowaways," he began—and got a laugh from everyone but the captain. "On behalf of Mr. Charley

Gross, the proprietor of Manhattan's famed Crystal Room, it is with pleasure that I welcome you to this very special moonlight cruise. Before the evening of festivities begins, I would like to introduce you to our honored guests. First, it gives me great pleasure to present the celebrated star of stage, screen, and television, Miss Judy Garland!"

The bandleader raised his hand and on the downswing, the musicians played a few bars of "Over the Rainbow." Judy stood up, left hand holding the arm of the chair to steady herself, and smiled, tilting her head in acknowledgment. All the guests, whether standing or seated, started to applaud. I stood there applauding, as well. When Judy once again took her seat, the ovation slowly died except for one person, who continued to clap enthusiastically. Renee nudged me until I stopped.

The bandleader then introduced the remaining special guests one at a time. For each person he presented, the band played an appropriate tune. The last to be introduced was Charley. "Last but not least," the bandleader continued, "is the man responsible for this evening's festivities. If it wasn't for his birth, we'd all be out on the town doing something more fun." A few nervous laughs followed. "Here he is, Mr. East Side himself. Won't you please rise and give a great big New York City round of applause to Mr. Char-r-l-e-e-y Gross!"

To the strains of "For He's a Jolly Good Fellow," Charley slowly entered the dining area, waving both hands and taking his time to acknowledge his guests. He shook hands and hugged women. As he approached the dais, he spotted me and, grinning broadly, pointed his index finger at me like a gun and quickly lowered his thumb like a trigger. I returned the gesture, reasonably sure that it was a good sign.

Sitting on his throne, Charley's dark shiny hair had a seductive appeal. His ever-present associates stood nearby and occasionally leaned over and whispered in his ear. Terry, in her black gown, dutifully supplied him with noshes. Mayor Lindsay also got his share of attention, mostly because his chair was a few feet from Judy's and guests had to pass him to reach her. Being a politician, of course, he was sure that they were seeking him out.

At last it was nine o'clock and we set sail. Most of the guests were either lined up at one of the bars or waiting to talk to Judy, who was flanked by the two golden boys who had been assigned to keep her supplied with whatever she needed. Tanya was working the male portion of the crowd, and Renee stood by the railing of the upper deck, taking in the fabulous view of the Manhattan skyline. At this point, Mayor Lindsay was conversing with the judge and taking in the fabulous view of the judge's busty date.

I just watched Judy, who was busily holding court with the throngs of guests who wanted to meet her. It was at the top of my priorities list to have a real conversation with my idol, but that would have to wait until an opportunity presented itself. In the meantime, all was going well.

🌴 🌴 🌴

Even before we had pulled away from the pier, the various bars, stationed throughout the ship, had opened, and they were continuously packed. This crowd included a lot of big drinkers, but since Charley had supplied the alcohol, I assumed there would be enough on board. He had also provided the ice for the drinks, so we had more ice than Admiral Bird had encountered on his expedition to the Antarctic.

Shortly after we embarked, the food stations opened and they, too, drew large crowds. These partygoers, though, were far more focused on keeping their glasses full than they were on loading their plates. Nonetheless, the food looked scrumptious, and on the pretense of making sure that the servers were doing their jobs, I sneaked a few bites for myself. Indeed, delicious.

Once the guests had been given time to fill their plates and glasses, the bandleader began introducing those people who had been selected to individually toast the guest of honor. One by one, each stood up and spoke about Charley. Some recalled funny anecdotes about their host, and others simply talked about how great he was and how much they loved him. I had never heard the words "swell guy" used so often in such a brief period of time, but I guess that was the overwhelming feeling about Charley. Mayor Lindsay, of course, threw in a few of his own political accomplishments, but that's what politicians do—they campaign.

At the end of the toasts, the bandleader introduced Judy Garland, who began heading toward the standing microphone on the small makeshift stage. On her way, Judy passed the ice sculpture of Charley, which, partially melted, now resembled the Penguin character in the Batman comics. As the crowd watched and applauded, I took Judy's arm and escorted her up the steps to the stage. Since I was to speak first, I grabbed the microphone.

"Shhhh!" I said, trying to quiet the guests. "People, it is my great pleasure and honor to present our very special guest, who has graciously agreed to sing a tribute to our host, Charley Gross. The most amazing singer of them all, the one and only Judy Garland!" The crowd's cheers resumed as I moved one of the chairs closer to Judy so she could steady herself. She had already enjoyed a number of drinks and looked as if she could use a little support.

As the band struck up, Judy held up her hand to silence the musicians. "John Wayne never sang," she said. "Bette Davis never sang. But I'm gonna sing for you. Is that okay with everybody?" The crowd responded with thunderous applause and foot stomping.

Judy sang "Get Happy" and "The Trolley Song," but soon everyone started shouting "Rainbow! Rainbow!" in unison. She signaled the band leader, and wow, she delivered "Over the Rainbow" with all her heart and soul. The applause was overwhelming. I was enthralled. Charley was beaming. The crowd shouted "More!" so she sang it again. As I watched, I thought back to that evening so many years ago when I had first seen her on screen and been struck by her unique voice, her heartfelt performance. I still was.

When Judy finished singing and began to leave the tiny stage, hordes of people approached her. She was used to crowd adulation, but she seemed to have a hard time standing up. A member of her entourage gripped her arm and led her back to her chair. The line did not abate; it simply grew longer, partially because of my own invited friends. I made sure to slip Renee into the line so she could meet Judy, too. Meanwhile, the lovely lady smiled, asked each person's name, and listened. *What a trooper,* I thought. Still, the situation was not exactly as I had imagined it. Judy Garland was sitting right in front of me, but there was nothing I could do to separate her from the throng and get her to myself—at least for now.

The party! Emerging from my Judy-induced trance, I remembered why I was there. I needed to see how things were progressing. Some of the guests were dancing to the music while others lined the railings, admiring the magnificent view as they nursed their drinks. I headed toward the lower deck where the carnival games were set up. They were the typical games where you try to toss a ring onto a bottle or throw a ball and knock over some stacked cans. A few of the more inebriated guests were throwing wildly, and in a couple of cases, a stray ball landed in the river. It didn't matter much as everyone appeared to be laughing and having a good time. Between the booze and the bobbing of the boat as it hit the river's waves, much of the crowd was a little wobbly, myself included.

🌴   🌴   🌴

About an hour after Judy finished her crowd-pleasing performance, I climbed to the top deck of the ship to find my sister, Renee. As I looked around at the colorful decorations, the busy servers, and the animated partygoers, I congratulated myself. The ship was as stunning as the expensively dressed guests, and the party was in full swing with nary a problem in sight. Or so I thought.

Suddenly, I heard violent shouting from the dining area beneath me. This was followed by further shouts, a series of crashes, and some high-pitched shrieks . . . one of which came from me. I literally froze in place. Given the number of Charley's macho friends and Mayor Lindsay's security personnel, how could any problem escalate to this level? I needed to find out.

As I ever so slowly approached the stairs, I was met by a number of guests and golden boys heading in the opposite direction. The staircase was narrow, and I couldn't fight the wave of people who ran up the steps. Impatiently, I waited for an opportunity to head down and find the source of the commotion. I certainly did not want to be part of any trouble, but as the person charged with running the party, I needed to show my face.

When I finally reached the dining area, it certainly looked as if there had been a fight of some sort. My golden chairs were scattered about and several tables were turned over. The ice sculpture, or what was left of it, was now a pile of crushed ice on the floor. I had known there could be problems with a party of this size. Even though the guest list had been carefully vetted by Terry, it was common for uninvited guests to slip in and for people to get invitations from those who couldn't attend. Of course, in this case, some of Charley's *invited* guests were characters you wouldn't want to meet in a dark alley—or a well-lit one, for that matter. Security was not part of my assignment. That task clearly seemed to fall into the capable hands of Charley's crew, which appeared to be absent from the scene.

It is remarkable how quickly people can scatter. The dining area on the second deck now seemed as empty as a graveyard, while intermittent shouts, hoots, and laughter could be heard on the upper and lower decks. And here I was, stuck in the middle, somewhere out on the Hudson River. Not knowing where to turn, I made my way towards the corner wall to right a dining table that had been turned on its side. I then received the jolt of my life. There, behind the upturned table, was Judy Garland seated quietly in a chair with a drink in her hand. This seemed beyond the realm of reality. And yet, there she was. Where the hell were her handlers? Where the hell was *anybody*?

"Hi," she said simply. "What's a nice guy like you doing in a place like this?" She didn't seem to recognize me, but appeared to be untroubled by the strange scene around her, almost as if nothing out of the ordinary had occurred. For a few seconds, I just stared as I tried to gather my wits. Fumbling for words, I asked her if she was all right.

"Am I all right? Oh, I will be after a couple more drinks," she quipped with a smile. "Why don't you pull up a chair and join me?"

"Miss Garland, where are your friends?" I asked, referring to the entourage that had accompanied her just minutes before. She pointed to the gold chair to her left, and I seated myself while she explained that she had no idea where they were. Earlier, she had slipped away to the ladies' room unnoticed, and when she emerged, she found the hall a wreck.

"So what's your name, sailor?" she teased gently.

"I'm Elliot Tiber. I'm a decorator. Well, normally I'm a decorator, but for now I'm the party planner—and this was not part of the plan," I explained. I quickly added that I was a big fan of hers, that her music had always meant so much in my life, and that her songs were always there for me when I was going through bad times. She smiled appreciatively. I had no idea what I was saying, but I was definitely on some type of roll. I told her that I had seen a couple of her concerts. "I was in the front row once and gave you roses. You took them and handed one back to me. I saved it in a book."

"So, are you Catholic?" she suddenly asked.

If any remark could stop me in my tracks, that was it. I responded instinctively, "Uh, no, I'm Jewish."

"My daughter Liza is Catholic. It's a beautiful religion, actually, the rituals. . . . So, are you married?"

"Aaah, actually, no, I'm an interior decorator." I had already stated what I did for a living, but this time, I trusted that she would get my full meaning.

"I had a decorator once, did everything in white . . . felt like I was living in a hospital."

"I much prefer black," I replied.

"Where are we going?" asked Judy.

"No place, really," I admitted.

"Then why are we on a boat?"

I explained that it was a birthday cruise for Charley Gross, the former director of the Department of Public Works, and that we were sailing around the island of Manhattan. As I continued to talk and get her up to speed, I placed my right hand gently on her left arm. Judy filled the silver screen in all her movies, but sitting next to her, she seemed small and vulnerable—not to mention unsteady.

"Do you know Charley?" I asked. Judy didn't reply. I doubted she knew him.

Taking a sip of her drink, she asked, "So, are you here alone?"

Smiling, I said, "I'm not alone now, Miss Garland. I'm with you."

"Y'know," she continued, "I'm always alone—no matter where I am, where I go, who I see. Makes no difference until that curtain goes up, and I know I have to go out there and start singing for my supper."

As she continued to speak, the dream-like quality of the situation kept occurring to me. It was like watching Judy being interviewed on TV—except that she was talking to me.

"What's your name? Give it to me again, would you, darling?" she implored.

"Elliot," I said. "My name is Elliot Tiber."

She chuckled in a knowing way. "That's the name you chose for yourself."

I felt my cheeks flush, sensing that she had met more than one "Eliyahu Teichberg" before in her travels.

"Yeah, well," I said, feeling a bit self-conscious, "I changed it from 'Teichberg'—it's better for business, you know. 'Tiber' sounds more. . . ."

"Chic?" she coyly interrupted.

Wow. This lady had me pegged in less than five minutes. I was a mere babe in the woods compared to Judy. But I felt more like I was being teased by an older sister than mocked by a superstar. In just a few minutes, I was starting to see a real person, not some Hollywood Dream Factory product. Despite her erratic manner—and several drinks—this woman was very quick, with a wicked sense of humor.

Judy asked if I had a place there in town, and I explained that I had a wonderful apartment—a sanctuary where I could truly be myself. "You can come live with me forever," I offered.

"Baby, let me tell you about home," Judy replied. "Home is whatever's in your suitcase and wherever you hang your hat. Contrary to the movie, it ain't in Kansas. Home is wherever you want it to be."

Just as I was about to ask her what she meant, two members of Judy's entourage appeared and discovered us seated in our own little world. The more massive of the bodyguards looked at her and then eyed me.

"She seems to be fine," I said. "We were just talking, and I . . ."

As I grasped for words, the guard placed his index finger on his lips, indicating that I should stop talking, which I did immediately. He then asked her if she was okay, and she playfully nodded yes.

The guard spoke in a very slow and deliberate manner. "Judy, we've been looking for you everywhere. One minute you were here and the next you were gone. Billy thought you were with me, and I thought you were with Billy. We met upstairs only to figure out you weren't with either of us. Judy, you shouldn't be here now . . . alone."

"I'm not alone. I'm with Elliot, the decorator," she said, lifting her glass.

Not amused, he continued. "We're going to get you off this boat as soon as it docks, and then we're going to take you home."

The animated expression disappeared from Judy's face. It was as if a curtain had fallen over the Judy I had been talking to only a few moments ago.

The man now turned to speak to me. "Uh, sir, would you please let go of Miss Garland's arm?" he said.

It was only then I realized that during our conversation, I had kept my hand on Judy's arm. It seemed that throughout my life, she was the one person to whom I had felt a true connection, and I just didn't want to let go.

"Home!" she said with a tight laugh as her entourage quickly gathered her up into a standing position. Judy blew a kiss in my direction, and they whisked her down the stairs. Even if she was never to remember my name—or even talking to me—I knew that I'd never forget the few minutes we had spent together, strange as they may have been.

🌴 🌴 🌴

For a short time, I had been unaware of what was happening around me on the ship. Now that Judy was gone, my mind again focused on the problem at hand.

I heard another commotion, much like the earlier incident. Only this time, the sound seemed to be coming from the upper deck. As I made my way to the staircase, a couple of my golden boys stopped and urged me to stay where I was. One of the boys had a bloody nose while the other had several cuts on his lips and below his eye. They explained that a bunch of guys were systematically throwing all the palm trees overboard to see if they would float. When they tried to stop them, they were met with fists and called "queers," among other things.

I felt bad for my boys. They were, after all, models, not fighters. I told them to find a bathroom and clean up. Angry and upset, I wanted to run up the stairs and command the goons to stop destroying my boat and my party—not to mention my career. But I knew better. Thirty years before, I had lost wrestling matches to my younger sister Renee—and to pretty much every other kid who had picked on me. As much as I wanted to play hero, I knew that it wouldn't work.

After a few minutes, I noticed that the yelling had been replaced by sounds of people mingling, laughing, talking. Cautiously, I climbed the stairs to the top level. When I reached the deck, I noticed that some of the bars were still standing, but others had been smashed, and several chairs looked broken as well. A large group of people had congregated near one of the railings. We had already passed the Statue of Liberty, so I wondered what had captured their attention. Making my way to the railing, I saw a half-dozen of my rented palms bobbing up and down in the moonlit waters of the Hudson. *I guess they do float after all,* I thought.

I turned away from the railing, picked up an overturned chair, and sat down. As unbelievable as it seemed, I had met Judy Garland and had even shared a few precious moments with her. On the other hand, my party—weeks and weeks of hard work—had been destroyed and there was nothing I could do about it.

As I sat there, Tanya and Renee approached me. Apparently, they had managed to find each other among the hordes of party-goers. Renee told me how thrilling it had been when the drunken goons had started a ruckus and Mayor Lindsay's plainclothes cops had sprung into action, hustling the mayor to safety. Lindsay's men then managed to tackle and round up the rowdy gang, who were now being contained on the lower deck until the boat docked.

Undaunted by the goons, the cops, the yelling and screaming, and the shattered furniture, Tanya looked at me and asked, "So, when are they serving dessert?" Oy vey.

Thirty minutes later, the party boat returned to the pier. All the bigwig guests—Lindsay, Charley, Terry, and the judge—disembarked first and ran to their waiting limousines. I think I even saw Terry and the birthday-cake blond holding hands as they slid into Charley's limo. Judy must have left the boat as well, but I didn't spot her or her entourage anywhere; it was as if they had disappeared the minute they left the dining area. Next off the boat were the inebriated men who had apparently started the brawl. Even from a distance, it was obvious that they had all been roughed up. Their jackets were ripped, their shirttails were hanging out, and they had been bloodied. Charley's personal security team pushed the men down the gangplank as the line of limos zoomed away. Within a few minutes, the drunks unceremoniously walked off into the night with Charley's security guys, surprisingly, just watching. They had beaten the crap out of the troublemakers and were now letting them go home.

Once the guests were off the boat, it was cleanup time for me and what remained of my crew. I had seen at least four of my golden guards bolt down the gangplank once we reached the pier, and I would have loved to run along with them. But no, it was my job to survey the damage and straighten things out to the best of my ability. So many chairs were missing, so many tables and bars had been broken and smashed, that it was more a matter of sorting the debris into reasonably neat piles.

Hours later, as my crew and I left the boat by way of the gangplank, the boat captain angrily made his way toward me. "Who in hell is responsible for this goddamn mess?" he demanded.

It was six in the morning and I was beyond tired. "I am just the party decorator," I explained. "I was instructed that any expenses incurred in the course of the trip would be covered by Charley Gross, the birthday boy himself."

"Are you sure about that, decorator man?" asked the captain, who had now been joined by the operator of the pier.

"Yes, I am. I was just to decorate the boat and come up with a theme for the party. The rest is up to Mr. Gross," I said, starting to feel a slight chill.

"Yeah," he said, with a wry smile. "I suppose it is, isn't it?" And with that, he walked back up the gangplank.

I told my crew that everyone would be paid for their work as soon as I received payment from Mr. Gross's organization. I then took an uptown subway to my apartment and just about managed to get myself into bed before I passed out for what would be the longest sleep of my life. Before falling into oblivion, I had three thoughts: I had met Judy Garland; I had thrown a disastrous party; and as soon as possible, I would have to visit Charley's Crystal Room to pick up my check. As it turned out, I was to sleep straight through the next day and not wake up until Sunday morning.

8

A Toll on the Road

Before I ventured into the Crystal Room, I wanted to be prepared. All that Sunday morning, I reviewed Charley's bill to make sure it was in order. The party expenses had run me a little over fifteen thousand dollars, with almost everything on credit. With an additional two thousand dollars for my services, the total came to seventeen thousand, a figure substantially less then Charley's original twenty thousand-dollar budget. To make sure that I could answer any questions that Charley might have about costs, I put together a breakdown of all the outstanding invoices. Normally, recordkeeping was not my strong point, but since there were so many bills, I had been careful about keeping the invoices straight. I wasn't certain how much the damaged and missing property would cost, but I would let Terry work that out with her suppliers. After all, how much could they charge for a fake palm tree?

When I arrived at the Crystal Room, I found Charley seated at his regular corner table with several of his favorite associates. Everyone was laughing and making jokes about some of the party guests. Although Terry had told me that I should never interrupt Charley when he was conducting business, I thought perhaps that, considering the jovial mood of the group, this might not be a bad time to present Charley with the bill. In fact, I was even feeling proud that, despite the lavish decór and the dazzling service, I had come in under budget. No matter what the palm trees cost, the party would be less than twenty thousand dollars. This was a good thing, or so I thought. But as I approached, the laughter ended abruptly and the mood at the table changed. Now all eyes were on me. Charley pushed his chair back, excused himself, and walked over to greet me.

"You want to speak to me, Elliot?" asked Charley.

"Well, yes. I have all of the bills from the party."

He looked me in the eyes and responded, "If I were you, I'd pay them quickly."

A bit confused, I asked when he was going to give me the money he owed me. Charley's face was emotionless. "I'm not giving you squat, Elliot. There were fights at my party. Terry slipped and hurt her ankle because there was crap all over the deck. There were a bunch of fags dressed in gold. Who the fuck are you to hire these guys, anyway?! I don't like queers, Elliot, and at this point, I'm not too crazy about you, either."

Charley made sure to speak loud enough for everyone at the table behind him to hear exactly what he was saying. I was stunned. I wasn't sure how to respond, but before I could say a word, Charley started to walk away, turning only to say, "Get the fuck out of here, Elliot. I don't ever want to see your faggot face again."

I must have stood there frozen for a long time, because one of Charley's bouncers eventually came over and signaled that I should head toward the door. Since the guy probably bench-pressed people larger than me at the gym, I thought it was prudent that I leave the club. I saw Terry as I left, but she immediately turned away, not wanting to make eye contact with me.

As I walked home, my shock turned to embarrassment. What the hell had just happened? Why did Charley turn on me? Okay, there had been a fight, but I didn't start it and I surely couldn't stop it. I wasn't the one in charge of security. He was. The more I thought about it, the more I realized that I had lived up to all my obligations. That asshole wasn't going to pay me because I was gay? Fuck him! I had done everything he asked for and more. There was no way I could afford to pay those party bills, and there was no way I was going to let this go.

Now, I was really getting angry, and I knew what I was going to do. I was going to sue Charley for the money. Over the years, I had sued clients on a couple of much smaller jobs, and I had won. This, however, was much more money, and Charley was much scarier than anyone I had ever dealt with before. But I had done nothing wrong. It was Sunday, so first thing Monday, I'd hire an attorney— or at least someone in law school.

🌴 🌴 🌴

That evening, back in my apartment, I tried to calm myself by watching TV. I was very upset about the sudden turn of events with Charley and kept mentally reviewing his excuses for not paying me. There were gays at the party. There were fights at the party. Terry had twisted her foot. Who was he kidding? I knew exactly why he wasn't going to pay me. I had dealt with homophobia before, but I wasn't going to give in. Maybe I couldn't stand up to his goons at the bar, but I could prevail in court.

It was one o'clock at night and I couldn't sleep. I needed something to drink that could calm me down. While alcohol might work for some people, I needed a big chocolate egg cream. So there I was, egg cream in hand, staring at the television. Channel 9 was running some black-and-white gangster movie from the 1950s. The tough guys in the film reminded me of the characters at the club.

An hour later, I had finally gone to bed when my doorbell rang. If it were someone from outside the building, the doorman would have first called up to let me know I had a visitor. Most likely, it was a neighbor with a problem, but it was a little late for that. I looked through the peephole and saw Charley's "associate" Neely Abruzzio standing outside my door. He looked as if he had stepped straight out of the movie I'd been watching on TV, except he was in color and very real. I'd seen Neely a number of times at the club. He seemed to have a permanent spot at the bar, never quite making it to a seat at Charley's table.

"Neely, it's late," I said. "Is there a problem? What do you want? How'd you get in?"

"Elliot, let me in. I gotta talk with you. It's about what happened at the club," he explained.

It was late, I was groggy, and I wasn't thinking too clearly. For a moment, I though that maybe Charley had had a change of heart and sent Neely over with the money, so I opened the door. "Come in," I said. "Let's sit down in the living room. Can I get you a drink or something?"

Walking in, Neely shook his head. He proceeded to sit on one of my oversized chairs and motioned for me to take a seat on the couch across from him.

"How did you get past the doorman?" I asked. That still didn't make sense to me.

Neely looked directly at me and said, "We belong to the same union."

What the hell does that mean? I thought. I wasn't about to ask him, though.

Charley's messenger proceeded to pull out a sheet of paper the size of a check. For a moment, I thought my nightmare was over. But when he held the paper in front of me, I could see it was a receipt that read "Paid in Full" for the amount of seventeen thousand dollars. Without missing a beat, Neely explained that, for accounting purposes, Charley wanted me to sign that everything he owed me had been paid up.

Completely missing the point, I explained that Charley had not paid me, so that nothing had been paid. Nothing *could* be paid until Charley gave me the money.

For the first time ever, I saw Neely smile. He explained that the bills would be paid in full as soon as I paid them, but that Charley needed to give this receipt to his accountant.

"But I don't have that kind of money," I explained.

"Look at this apartment, Elliot. You ain't gonna have a problem finding it," said Neely, almost in a whisper. "Listen, I don't think you're stupid, but you've been comin' in and outta the club for months. It ain't no social club that Charley and his partners are runnin'. It's a big family business, and I'm part of the family."

With that, Neely pulled open the jacket of his gray sharkskin suit and exposed a holster that held a large gun. I began to tremble uncontrollably as everything became suddenly, horribly clear. Neely was no security guard, bodyguard, or cop. He was a mobster. Did that mean that Charley was a mobster, as well, along with all his associates? I couldn't quite accept it. It just didn't make any sense.

"But Charley's Jewish," I protested. "It's Charley *Gross.*"

Neely seemed slightly amused, but only for a moment. "Look, Elliot," he said, "normally, it goes like this. I come in, I may have to break somethin' to get your attention, and I'm not talkin' about furniture. But right now, I ain't got nothin' against you. You're okay. You're like my little brother, Nunio. He's a finocchio too, y'know, but that don't mean he's not a good person. Nobody in my family talks to him being a finoc and all, but I still love him."

I found it both terrifying and strange for a gangster to take the time to admit something like this to a guy whom he could calmly kill. He quickly frowned and continued, "So here's the deal. I got a job to do here, and you're it. It's like this, Elliot. Charley says either you sign the receipt, or I'm gonna have to hurt you. And if you still don't wanna sign the bill paid-in-full . . . well, let's just say they may find you out there floatin' in the river with those fuckin' palm trees. You get my drift, Elliot? It's up to you, pal," he said, reaching out to hand me a pen.

The image of me and the palm trees floating down the Hudson River was more than enough to get me to sign. I grabbed the pen and tried desperately to write my name. My hand was trembling but I managed to steady it long enough to scrawl something that looked like my signature across the receipt. "Make sure you write 'Paid in Full' under your name," he ordered.

Neely stood up quickly, took the receipt out of my hand, and placed it in his coat pocket. "See how easy this is? Nobody has to get hurt." He paused for a moment and added, "You wanna pay Charley's people real soon. Some of those guys you rented from— they don't like to be kept waitin'."

I just wanted Neely out of my home. He took a few steps towards the entryway, and stopped. Turning to face me, he said, "Y'know, this is a really nice apartment you got here." And with that, he left.

After closing and locking my apartment door, I sank to the floor, where I sat for at least an hour. *How could I have been so stupid?* I kept asking myself. The only guys who would wear sharkskin suits and loud silk ties had to be thugs and mobsters. And then, even before I considered my own plight, my thoughts wandered to poor Tony, my ex-boyfriend, the maître d'. *What the hell did they do to him?* I wondered.

Now it was all falling into place. No wonder Terry never talked about anything other than the menu and the entertainers. No wonder Charley had so many private meetings. No wonder some of the patrons carried guns and everyone stopped talking whenever I got within earshot. I started to imagine some of the gruesome details I could have overheard. Oy!

Even if I did go to court and claim that I was forced to sign off on a receipt for my services, there was a really good chance that I could be made to disappear just like Tony. The fact was that I had no way of paying fifteen thousand dollars, not counting my own two thousand-dollar fee, which I could now kiss good-bye. I had a total of about two thousand dollars in the bank—enough to keep the hotel going for a couple of months at best. My thoughts were racing. Lawyers may have been out, but I knew a judge. Of course! All I had to do was call Judge Susskind the next morning and tell him what was going on. If anybody could help me, he would be the one. I'd have to let him know that his friend Charley was associated with the mob, but in his position as a judge, I'd be doing him a favor. It was all so unbelievable.

After the late-night visit from Neely, sleeping was out of the question. I spent the rest of the night finishing off everything in the refrigerator as I visualized Neely pulling out his gun and shooting me. Good thing he liked me.

First thing in the morning, I telephoned the good judge and explained all about Charley and Terry and the palm trees and their not wanting to pay the seventeen thousand-dollar bill. I must have sounded like a babbling idiot. I told him about Neely Abruzzio's frightening visit, and how I had been forced to sign a receipt for money that I had never received. I finally stopped, hoping that the judge could tell me what I should do next.

There was a long silence. I could actually hear my heart beating as I held the telephone receiver to my ear, waiting for a response. Finally, the judge spoke.

"Look, Elliot," he said. "I'm somewhat pressed for time and I don't really know what's going on. However, what I can tell you is that it would be highly inappropriate for me to get involved. As a friend, I advise you to simply write it off as a business expense. It would be prudent of you to simply absorb the loss and avoid any further after-midnight meetings with the gentlemen who hang around the Crystal Room." He then wished me good luck, sent regards from Rose, and hung up.

I was speechless. Clearly, the judge wasn't going to be of any help. Maybe he wanted to stay clear of the mess, maybe he was as scared of Charley's associates as I was, or—was it even possible?—maybe he was one of them. Perhaps the judge was as crooked as Charley. No wonder every time I took Rose shopping, everyone treated us so well. Susskind was probably part of the mob, too. Could Mayor Lindsay be one of them, as well? And to think that I had voted for that handsome son of a bitch.

I stayed in my apartment for what felt like days, although it was only a matter of hours. All the manic events of the past few days were starting to play with my head. I felt dizzy, nauseous, alone, and scared. Everything that had ever happened in my life seemed fake and real at the same time. Everyone's face and name seemed to turn into the same name—*them*. Could it be that every person I had ever met in New York City was in on this? Worse yet, had Momma been right? Was I simply a loser who was forever doomed to failure and humiliation?

By evening, I had convinced myself that Neely had bugged the apartment and that Charley and the others had heard every word of my phone call to the judge. Either that or the good judge had called Charley and told him about our conversation. The silence in my apartment was deafening. I needed to hear something or someone—music. I walked over to the jukebox and turned it on, filling the apartment with Judy Garland's sweet, reassuring voice. I sat in the music room for hours, clutching a pillow and hoping this would all go away. Finally, I fell asleep.

🌴　🌴　🌴

The warm light of the morning sun slipped through curtains onto my face. I awoke, still feeling exhausted. The paranoia that had set in the day before may have been a reaction to my lack of sleep. Then again, it may have simply been justified. The fact was that I was in a terrible situation—terrible and potentially deadly. What the hell were my options? I needed a lot of money and needed it fast. There was no way that the sum I had in the bank could get me out of this mess. No matter what, I had to pay my rent and throw money into that upstate hotel. Perhaps I should just run away and hide. Maybe in a few months—or a few years—all the suppliers and caterers would forget about the money I owed them. Or maybe Neely or one of his cohorts would come looking for me and I'd end up at the bottom of White Lake.

I had told Terry pretty much everything about my life while hanging out at the club. They'd know where to find me. Even if I hid out in the barn behind the motel, I could be sure that Momma would point them in my general direction. "That rotten no-good-nik son of mine? You'll find him in the back. Before you shoot him, maybe you want some cholent—a sandwich, maybe?"

Okay, so running away was not an option. I was going to have to pay these bills, all of them, in full. No wonder Charley had told me to use his name when I was planning the party, but then had me sign my name when I ordered the decorations. What an idiot I had been. Rule Number One in interior decorating: Always let the client pay for everything in advance. What had I been thinking? But thoughts like this were not going to get me out of this jam. I had to stop beating myself up—that's what Momma was for.

Since I had dropped all my other jobs to concentrate on Charley's party, there was no way I could make fifteen thousand dollars through decorating assignments. It would take me weeks to bring in new business and even longer to get paid. What I needed was some fast money. And then it occurred to me: I knew lots of rich non-gangster-type folks who had money to burn. I could borrow a little from each of them and arrange to pay it back when I could. Better yet, I could work off the money by offering my services free of charge. Who doesn't want their own successful interior decorator at their beck and call? I had found a way out.

🌴　🌴　🌴

I looked at my watch. It was nine o'clock in the morning, Tuesday or Wednesday; I wasn't too sure. I sat at my antique desk, pulled out my Rolodex, and started to pore over the cards of friends, lovers, clients—anyone with whom I'd been in contact over the past few years. *Focus*, I thought to myself. Who should I call first? The choice was obvious: Curtis Murray, the man who had first brought me into the business and helped me develop my career. I quickly flipped to the M's, but with my organizational skills, I found his name under H. I held my breath as I dialed the number. Knowing he was a late-night partier, I thought it might be a little early for Curtis, but I knew he would understand.

"Hello," said a demure and decidedly gender-neutral voice on the other end.

"Hi, is Curtis there? This is his friend Elliot Tiber."

"Who?" the voice asked.

"Elliot . . . Elliot Tiber. Curtis knows me. We've worked together lots of times," I said, sounding a bit desperate. "Is Curtis there?"

"No, Mr. Tiber, Curtis is out of town and won't be back for at least three weeks. He's in Europe on business. Is there something I can do, or would you like to leave a message?" The voice sounded cool, calm, detached.

I knew of no dignified way to leave word that I needed money, especially since I had barely communicated with my mentor since my own business had begun to thrive. On the other end, the voice said that if I left my number, it would be given to Curtis when he called in, which would probably be in a week or two. Feeling defeated, I halfheartedly recited my phone number and hung up the phone.

Okay, let's not panic yet, I told myself. All I needed to do was sound calm, not too pushy or desperate. And I should definitely avoid crying.

I would start with the A's and work my way straight through the alphabet. That way, I wouldn't miss anyone. The first name in the A's was Peter Doyle—perhaps because he had been living in the Ansonia, a fabulous building on Central Park West, when I met him. We had been good friends and then lovers. He had inherited a group of valuable parking lot properties throughout the city, and also owned a piece of a Broadway theater. I called his office number and asked to be connected. I waited a moment, and then heard Peter's cheerful voice: "Hello, this is Peter, can I help you?"

"Hi, Peter, this is Elliot. I just called to say. . . ." That's when I heard a loud click, and the line went dead. *Oh shit, that's right,* I thought to myself. That relationship hadn't ended very well because I had messed around with his twin brother "by mistake."

I called three more numbers but each time, got no answer. I pulled the cards out of the Rolodex and arranged them in a neat pile alongside the phone. This would be my "people to call back later" group.

Jonathan Bausch was my next call. He had a showroom in the D&D Building, where he sold carpets and rugs. I had steered many of my clients his way over the years.

"Well, hello, Elliot, how are things?" asked Jonathan. He sounded cheerful and genuinely happy to hear from me. Suddenly, I felt hopeful.

"Jonathan, hi!" I said, trying very hard to match his level of sunny optimism. I told him that I was working really hard to maintain and build the business, and that I was still certain to tell clients about all the excellent items he could provide.

"You've always been helpful with clients," he said, sounding sincere. "I appreciate it."

An awkward pause followed as I tried to think of something, anything, to say to buy more time. I dreaded telling him my true reason for calling.

"So, what can I do for you today, Elliot? Need a rug?"

"No, it's not that, Jonathan," I said, trying to keep my voice even and the rhythm of my words from sounding too fast or too slow. "It's just that in trying to expand the client base, I've fallen a little behind on some of my business expenses. I'm a bit . . . overextended right now." This was harder than I thought it would be. "I just need a little help to keep things going."

Jonathan said that he understood completely about having to fill holes here and there, and he knew I was good for a loan. Then he asked the question that I dreaded most.

"How much do you need, Elliot?"

"Well, uh," I said, clearing my throat. "I think that I could get everything in place again with about two . . . two . . . or maybe three thousand dollars. You know I'm good for it."

Silence, and then more silence.

It dawned on me that I really had to pee. Soon, I felt so desperate that I heard myself offering Jonathan a weekend at the White Lake motel. He interrupted.

"Gee, Elliot, that's a lot of money you're asking for." Little did he realize it was only a fraction of what I owed.

"I know, Jon," I said, trying to sound a little more personal, more intimate. "It's really only a temporary thing. And with all the jobs I've got lined up, I should be able to pay you back in a few months. I'll also be bringing a lot of clients into your place, of course."

"Elliot," Jonathan said, sounding like a doctor who has to tell a family member that a loved one has just died, "I just don't have that kind of money to lend. All I've got is tied up in the business, and there's just no way that I can shake any of it loose right now. I'm really sorry, Elliot." And he sounded like he meant it.

"Well, I understand your situation, Jon," I said, sounding like I meant it, too. "I'll try to see what I can do on my end. I'll still tell folks that they should come to see you, okay?" My voice began to crack as I tried to save face.

"You got it, Elliot," he said. "And I certainly hope you can figure things out."

With that, another phone call ended. I was only up to the second of twenty-six letters of the alphabet, but had begun to suspect that my plan was ludicrous. And I still had to pee.

For three hours, I doggedly made call after call and was met with busy signals, phones that rang off the hook, and refusals that ranged from blunt to awkwardly polite. "Sorry, Elliot." "Wish I could help, Elliot." "I was actually going to call *you* for money, Elliot." The bottom line was that I wasn't getting any help in meeting my bottom line, and with every call, the noose around my neck tightened a bit more. By the time I had worked my way to the middle of the Rolodex—and had no luck reaching Anna McKenna, a former Hunter College teacher—I realized that this just wasn't working. And I still had to pluck fifteen thousand dollars out of the air.

Growing ever more frantic, I began to sift through my memories, hoping to dredge up someone, anyone, who might be of help. Gregory Rossov, the man who had hired me to work at Sloane's, must have moved away because his number was no longer in service. I thought of my old radio show-biz friend, Bea Kalmus, but then recalled that Mother Kalmus was in charge of all Bea's finances and was as tight with cash as Momma had always been.

And then I remembered Lou and Erica Shapiro, who had been so kind to me years before. A smile crossed my lips for the first time in days as I recalled how nice it had been to spend time with them and their teenage son as I redecorated their home and, afterwards, was welcomed as a member of the family. They had enabled me to quit the Detroit Furniture job and become a full-time interior decorator. Perhaps, without knowing it, they had also given me the support that I had never received from my actual family.

Hurriedly, I skipped ahead to the letter S, found the Shapiros' number, and twirled my index finger into the rotary phone seven times. The phone rang . . . and rang . . . and rang. There was no answer. It seemed strange that they would not pick up the phone around dinnertime since they usually ate at home. With my luck, they were probably traveling with Curtis somewhere in Europe. In case they weren't, I placed their card on top of the growing stack on my desk. I would continue to call them, but at that moment, my failure to reach them felt like a sign.

About twenty minutes later, my phone rang—and I jumped about two feet in the air. Maybe it was someone actually returning my call, or maybe it was one of Charley's associates. On the third ring, I worked up the courage to answer. After all, Charley's cronies really weren't interested in having a chat. Their approach was a little more direct.

"Hello?" I said, warily.

"Elliot?! It's Renee. Are you okay? I've been calling all day, but your line has been busy!"

I was so happy to hear from my baby sister that I could have cried—and I did. With all that had happened, we hadn't had a chance to talk since the party. I figured my sister didn't have connections with the mob, so for the next twenty minutes, I told her everything that had unfolded since the night of the event. When I explained that Charley was not going to pay the bills, she said that she just couldn't believe it.

"Look, Elliot," she said, "I know it's not much, but I've got over two hundred dollars saved up that I could give you. Would that help?"

I could feel the tears well up in my eyes. I tried to speak, but the words didn't come. After a few moments, I cleared my throat. "Thanks, but no thanks, sis," I said. "That's very nice, but it's my responsibility. I got myself into this mess and I'll get myself out."

Maybe it was an older brother's need to protect the baby of the family, or maybe it was my sense of pride, but I couldn't bring myself to state the actual sum I owed. It was just too devastating. In my family, the words "I love you" were rarely, if ever, offered. I thanked Renee for listening to my story and ended the conversation with, "I love you, sis."

Four hours and thirteen unlucky Rolodex letters later, I found myself right back where I started—still sick with worry. What I couldn't figure out was whether I was more frightened that some of the people who I owed money would come after me, or more disappointed that there was no one in my professional or social life that I could count on to help me out. Physically and mentally, I was exhausted. I couldn't make another call; I didn't want to make another call. Plan A wasn't working. I needed Plan B and I needed it fast. Problem was, I had no Plan B.

�palm🌴🌴

The music floated in softly from the music room. I had been sitting in my dining room for hours, my head resting on my arms and my body slumped forward on the table. In my head, I had gone through dozens and dozens of scenarios. The common theme was simple: I would stall any creditors that could be stalled, and pay those who were unwilling to wait. While this strategy wouldn't do much for my reputation, it would buy me time. But how would I know which people I could put off without getting a knock on the door in the middle of the night? Worse yet, how would I pay those I couldn't stall? However I played it out, I knew one thing for sure: This was the worst thing that had ever occurred in my rapidly disintegrating life. Never before had cleaning toilets at the motel in White Lake looked so good.

My neck hurt, my throat was sore, my eyes were burning, and my stomach was making noise. The fridge was pretty much empty, so cereal would have to do. I rose from my chair and yawned, arching my back and neck to work out the kinks. When I opened my eyes, I was looking at the Austrian crystal chandelier over my head. It was beautiful—beautiful and rare and . . . very, very expensive. And then it dawned on me: The money I needed was all around me! I had nine rooms filled with antiques, crystal chandeliers, vases, and all sorts of chachkas. It had taken me years to put together the collection of goodies in my over-the-rainbow apartment. If I sold enough of it off, I could make the money I needed to get out of this mess.

As an interior designer, I knew that the best place to sell off an item of value was an auction. Whenever well-to-do clients needed mad money, they would auction off one of their lesser pieces for top dollar. Unfortunately, with the threat of violence looming so close, there was no time to organize an auction because it normally took months for a reputable house to set one up. The best I could do was arrange for their in-house appraisers to view my furnishings and buy them directly from me with the idea that they could later auction them off. Sure, they'd pay me less money than I would make at an auction, but time was of the essence.

The thought of selling off my wonderful treasures was more than upsetting. Over the years, my apartment had come to define me. It was a symbol of my success and my creation of a new and better life, far, far away from my Bensonhurst beginnings. I could not let myself think about that now, though—not if I wanted to avoid becoming fish food at the bottom of the Hudson. The choice was simple: Stay alive in an emptied apartment, or get killed in a beautifully furnished flat. Sure, the obituary would probably be accompanied by some marvelous photos of my home, but I figured that living was still the better option.

It was about six in the evening. As a rule, most New York City auction houses stay open late. With cereal bowl in hand, I made my way back to the Rolodex and started calling the auction house contacts I had made over the years. I explained that I was moving in a few days and could not possibly take all of my valuable items with me. To make the situation seem a little more urgent, I mentioned that Sotheby's—the most prestigious auction house in Manhattan— was sending someone over the next afternoon. Within an hour or so, a few of the more competitive houses had agreed to visit the next morning. I even convinced Sotheby's to come by, claiming that Christie's had shown an interest in my collection.

The next day, as each buyer made his way through the rooms, I tried to put a spin on every item by explaining how it had been owned by royalty or how it had survived war or foreign invasion. Momma would have been proud, but the appraisers responded by rolling their eyes, smirking, or simply saying, "I don't think so." These people knew bullshit when they heard it. The premier auction houses would take only the higher-quality items. My beloved jukebox was easily worth fifteen hundred dollars at the time, even without all the Judy LPs that I removed before selling it. Now more than ever, I knew that I'd need Judy to help me survive. Two auction house representatives wanted the jukebox, which helped drive up the price. Even so, I wound up bringing in about nine hundred dollars for the vintage piece.

One by one, visitors made their offers known, and deals were struck. A set of four crystal Swarovski sconces went for two hundred dollars, while a gold-trimmed antique china service for twenty-four garnered four hundred. Four oriental room-size rugs—authentically Persian, but not antique—brought in around six hundred and fifty bucks each. The twelve dining room chairs went for about three hundred dollars each. My own dining room table creation, built on a base of six carousel horses, brought in one thousand dollars. It had cost me only three hundred dollars to construct, including carpenter fees. The crème de la crème, though, was the crystal chandelier from the floor of B. Altman's. Studded with Swarovski crystals, it was worth close to twelve thousand dollars and brought in another six grand.

When the last auction house appraiser had made the last offer, I totaled my take and found that I had made almost the entire sum needed to pay Charley's bills. I had another two thousand dollars in the bank, but knew that I'd need more money if I were to pay the bills upstate. Truth be told, Momma was nearly as scary as the mob, and just like Charley's boys, she knew where to find me.

All my lovely furnishings were leaving me on hand trucks, in boxes, and in the arms of giddy auction house employees who knew they had gotten great deals. I could still remember the excitement I had experienced when finding each piece, bringing it home, fixing it up, placing it in the perfect spot. I had spent so much time creating my ideal home, and now my beautiful rainbow was being taken away.

🌴　🌴　🌴

With auction house checks in hand, I literally ran to the bank so I could make my deposits before closing time. It would take a week for the checks to clear, so the creditors would have to wait just a little bit longer. And I still had the nagging thought that Charley and his gang had it in for me. Since I knew who he was and I could identify his so-called associates, perhaps they assumed that I knew everything they were up to—despite the fact that I had remained clueless for so many months. I had seen all too many late-night movies in which some poor sap pays off the money he owes, and the mobsters still kill him so he can't talk. Maybe these were a higher class of mobsters; maybe they weren't. All I knew was that I was scared and depressed, and wanted nothing more than to pay off the bills and drop off everyone's radar.

A week later, when the checks had cleared, I ran from rental company to rental company, from caterer to baker, dropping off checks and making sure to get a signed receipt in return. By week's end, I had managed to pay everyone except the props rental company, which was my own contact. They had already called twice, and each time, I had told them I was running out the door but would be in touch with them shortly. Unfortunately, I didn't know how much they were going to charge me per tree, but I figured that I needed a few thousand dollars more than I had managed to make through the auction houses.

I decided that my best bet was to have a yard sale. Since outdoor yards were hard to come by in Manhattan, the sale would be held in my apartment. I spread the word, inviting as many people as I could. They may not have been interested in lending me money, but they knew exactly what a bargain was. My sale would be in two days' time, on a Saturday, when everyone would be home from work.

🌴 🌴 🌴

And so it was on a tranquil Saturday morning in June 1968 that I, Elliot Tiber, held a yard sale in my posh Upper West Side apartment. Considering that I had spent the last few months working for the judge and Charley, I hadn't seen some of these people in a while. Many of my acquaintances didn't show up, and those who did were full of questions. Why was I selling? Was I leaving the business? Was I moving? Since I didn't want to arouse suspicion, I simply explained that my parents weren't doing well. Bad health, bad business, bad motel, bad breath—whatever. The point was that Momma and Pop really needed me and I was going to help them out. Renee and Tanya were the only ones to whom I confessed some version of the truth. Tanya, who wasn't told about the mob connection, expressed her sympathy. Renee was still frightened for me and suggested that I move up to White Lake, just to be safe. Apparently, she and I watched the same gangster movies. I told her not to worry; I'd figure out something soon.

The Saturday sale went better than I would have imagined. Along with most of the remaining large pieces and many small items, I sold several of my own paintings along with some paintings purchased years before from up-and-coming Greenwich Village artists. The last item to go was my beloved barber chair—the only piece of furniture that remained from my first apartment. By late evening, I had made a few thousand bucks. I just hoped that this would cover both the palm trees and all the upcoming bills at White Lake.

"How could you lose every tree?! What the hell is wrong with you?! What are you, some kind of fucking idiot?!"

All valid questions, I thought, as the owner of the props rental company proceeded to call me every name in the book. "Do you know how much money this is costing me in lost rentals?!!" he screamed as he began totaling up what I owed. All I kept thinking was, *How big a demand could there be for fake palm trees?* Of course, considering his mood, I dared not ask.

After what seemed like hours of watching the irate man write down numbers, cross them out, and write down more numbers, he handed me an itemized bill for all that had been lost in the waters of the Hudson. I almost choked. It would have been cheaper for me to go down to Miami Beach, buy real trees, and ship them up to New York. Nonetheless, I kept my mouth shut and wrote out a check. From the original four hundred-dollar rental fee, the price had ballooned to eighteen hundred dollars. Luckily, I had made enough at the sale to cover it—although barely—and had a little left over to throw into White Lake.

The props shop was located on Thirty-Eighth Street and Eighth Avenue. It was a beautiful day in Manhattan, and all of my debts had been paid off, so I decided to walk the forty-eight blocks back to my apartment. The last two weeks had been crazy. My life had been threatened, the people I thought I could count on had turned away from me, and the home that had taken me nearly ten years to create had been dismantled and sold. My world was in limbo, and I had no idea what to do. At the sale, I had told everyone that I was going to give my folks a hand, but I hadn't really meant it. The more I thought about it, though, the more I realized how limited my options were.

Two hours later, I found myself in the elevator heading up to my apartment. As I entered the marble foyer, the front door slammed shut behind me, the sound reverberating through the empty rooms. Scattered around were assorted items that no one had wanted to buy. My dining room was empty, the jukebox was gone, most of the walls were bare, and even my barber chair was no longer there. The only sound I could hear was me, knocking the back of my head against the wall. The loneliness and desperation I felt were palpable and cut me like a serrated knife. What was I going to do? It was one thing to go up to White Lake for a weekend and return to a beautiful home in the city. It was quite another to return to an empty shell. Then and there, I decided that I had to leave the apartment—or, more accurately, to escape to a place that would make me invisible. Maybe being invisible was my destiny.

Within a couple of days, I had packed my few remaining possessions, including my Judy albums, my clothes, my portfolio, and some odds and ends from the past ten years. I skipped out of the apartment in the middle of the night and left no forwarding address. As I drove away from my life on Eighty-Sixth Street, towards the White Lake nightmare that waited on the other end of the New York Thruway, my paranoia was in high gear. Every time I stopped at a traffic light or paid a highway toll, I looked around, expecting a mobster to appear, gun in hand, and shoot me in cold blood. Martin Luther King, Jr. had been assassinated a few months earlier, in April, and Robert F. Kennedy had been shot dead only the week before. I remember thinking, *If I were killed, who would give a fuck about a faggot decorator floating in the Hudson River?* Consumed with both bitterness and failure, I drove toward my self-imposed exile.

9

Back to White Lake

Kutsher's, Brickman's, the Concord, Grossinger's—billboards for these resorts dotted the roadside along Route 17B. Judging from the exuberant ads, you would never guess that, for the most part, the golden age of these Catskill hotels had long since passed, but it had. As I drove to White Lake, I thought, *Well, at least they had a golden age.* It was not like the continuing downward spiral that gripped my parents' motel—and my life. I had taken this road to the motel at least a hundred times, but this time, it felt different. I felt different. All of the passion for my career, my art, and my life had been sucked out of me. The pot of gold at the end of the rainbow, which only a few months earlier seemed well within my grasp, had disappeared, just as I was disappearing now.

It was early in the morning, and I definitely needed a restroom stop. I pulled into the Red Apple Rest, a twenty-four-hour Jewish pit stop that marked the halfway point between the city and the all-too-familiar hell of the motel. I walked into the men's room, entered a stall, sat down, and cried my eyes out. I felt that I no longer had the head, the heart, or the courage to go back to the work I had loved to do in Manhattan. The worst part was that I couldn't help thinking that maybe Momma had been right when she told me that I would screw up my life and end up with nothing. Twenty minutes and two egg creams later, I was back behind the wheel of my car.

As I navigated the long, winding mountain roads, it occurred to me that it might be better to drive straight off one of those steep cliffs than to hear Momma say, "I told you so! I told you so! I told you so!" On the other hand, why should I kill myself when my reason for fleeing the city was to avoid being killed? Besides, it would probably hurt a lot and ruin a well-coordinated outfit, and I was too big a coward anyway. So I drove on.

I arrived at the motel at about eight in the morning. Because it was a weekday, my parents were surprised to see me. They were just opening up the coffee shop when they saw me pull into the parking lot.

"Look who's here, Jack!" Momma shouted. "Something's the matter. He never comes here before the weekend! What, you couldn't call to say you were coming?!"

"And I'm glad to see you too, Momma," I responded. "Hi, Pop," I said to my father. He looked even more haggard and tired than the last time I'd seen him. "Is the shop already open?" I asked.

My father said, "Come in, we'll be ready in a few minutes. Come sit at the counter." Pop never spoke much or showed much emotion, but he was clearly glad to be speaking to someone other than Momma.

As I sat down, I saw that my mother was looking directly into my face from across the counter. "Elli," she said, "you look terrible. More than the usual. Here, you'll eat something! Have some orange juice. I'll heat up the waffles." Thankfully, Momma made her greasy cholent dish only for lunch or dinner.

Exhausted by all that had happened in recent days, I made a deliberate decision to lie to my parents. I told them that after thinking about it, I wanted to help run the motel. Coming up only on weekends wasn't working. Maybe if I spent more time in White Lake, I could turn things around. I explained that the interior decorating business was usually slow during the summer, and the cost of the motel was getting out of hand.

I really didn't think that the story about Charley, the club, the party, meeting Judy Garland, and losing dozens of rented palm trees would make any sense to my parents. Hell, it still didn't make sense to me. Being able to bare my soul to Renee some days earlier had given me some solace. Telling those same troubles to Momma and Pop would only aggravate my situation. Besides, I actually half believed that Momma would call Charley and his guys and tell them that her no-good, non-rabbi son was up at the motel—especially if she thought that a cash reward was being offered.

Although I did everything I could to make the words "I'm here to help with the motel" sound convincing, it seemed that Momma could sense that something was not right. That was probably what had prevented the Cossacks from catching her back in Russia. She squinted her eyes, folded her arms, turned to Pop, and said, "You see, Mr. Big Shot isn't such a big shot! Now he wants to help us clean toilets and make beds full-time? Something's not right. Something happened." And then, as if she had divined the true story from Moses himself, she turned to me and proclaimed, "Eliyahu, you were fired! I knew it. You couldn't keep a job. You see, you could have been a rabbi or at least a dentist like I told you . . . but no, did you listen?!"

I let her go on and on and on. I wasn't sure what job she thought I had been fired from, but I didn't have the will or energy to argue. If it wasn't my own miserable life she was screaming about, I might have laughed at her ongoing rant, but maybe there was some truth to it. Pop, as usual, said nothing.

For the rest of the Catskill resorts, the Memorial Day weekend traditionally marked the beginning of the summer season. For us, however, it was the Fourth of July. That was because we barely had any business until the Fourth of July. The truth was that in preparing for yet another championship Teichberg season, my dad could use another pair of hands on a more regular basis. I figured that if I worked with him rather than Momma, life would be tolerable. I knew that he was not going to ask any questions.

Once my mother realized that I wasn't talking back, she stopped her raving. At that moment, it occurred to me that this was probably why my father had adopted the same tactic years before. So I listened and said nothing . . . much like a prisoner of war. I ate the food that was placed in front of me, said "Thank you," and asked if I could have the "deluxe room" to stay in for just a few days. Of course, "deluxe" did not refer to any actual lap of luxury. At our motel, this term referred to any room that had a TV set, running water, and a bar of soap. At Momma's insistence, towels were always extra, and the TV didn't have to work. I was miserable and wanted nothing more than to be left alone—especially by Momma.

My father quietly said, "Take room number 27, Elli. Nobody's staying there now, and the door's open." Momma added, "I'm telling you now that you'll move to your own room as soon as the season starts."

Although I doubted that the season would ever really "start," I was glad to have some privacy. For the next five days, I slept, I ate, and I watched television in number 27. To most people, such activity from an adult might have been a sign that there was something wrong; my parents, however, initially adjusted to my behavior just fine. Occasionally, my isolation was interrupted by Momma's complaints that I was a bad son who wasn't helping them with the motel and who *still* wasn't married. In the state I was in, I didn't have the energy to point out that they wouldn't even *have* their motel if I hadn't been sending them money to pay the bills, nor would they have an upcoming summer season if I hadn't sold off everything in my Manhattan home. And I was never going to get married.

And so it was that on the fifth day of my White Lake funk, I emerged from deluxe room number 27—with a little encouragement from Momma, of course. "Eliyahu! We have customers who want this room," Momma had yelled through the door. "And your father needs help making some signs!"

Of course, I didn't believe there *were* any customers who wanted this particular room. However, I didn't want Pop to do all the work by himself. Pop seemed to have slowed down quite a bit since I last saw him. Momma, on the other hand, moved from chore to chore with boundless energy. It was like watching the Road Runner with a Russian accent.

At around noon, I found my father repainting signs in the barn. I told him that since I was now working at the motel full-time, I would be in charge of all signs. He looked at me, said "Good," handed me the brush, and left. He was definitely a man of few words. Although over the years, I had sometimes visited during the winter months, I had made it a habit to work at the motel each weekend of the summer season. And as hard as I tried to make a go of the place, I obviously wasn't succeeding.

Now that I was going to be a more permanent part of this business, I needed to make a fresh start, and what better way to make a new start than to rename the motel? I had plenty of ideas. I had considered renaming it the Bates Motel, and while that would have been funny, it might have been a bit too creepy. Nobody would ever use the showers, not that all of them worked anyway, but most likely, the name would have discouraged even the few lost or drunken tourists that we did attract. Perhaps the Crystal Room Motel would have attracted mobsters and their families. But no, they apparently didn't like to pay their bills. I considered Grossinger's Two, assuming people would think it was connected to Grossinger's in some way. Of course, the real Grossinger family would not have been pleased. And then it came to me. Our sign would read "El Monaco" in homage to the small European enclave where the beautiful American movie actress Grace Kelly now resided as a princess. I always liked her in *To Catch a Thief,* although I think I liked Cary Grant better. This name change would mark the birth of a new and better motel. Yes, my parents would be running it the way they always had, but the business would have new signs and a glamorous new identity.

🌴 🌴 🌴

For the last eight years, whenever I had gone up to the motel, I had created an alter ego for myself. In New York City, I was outgoing, funny, loud, and definitely into men. When I was up at White Lake, however, I was the dutiful son who followed the orders that my mother barked out, tried to come up with ideas that would help the motel turn a profit, and kept myself a relatively blank slate in terms of sexuality. No one knew that I was gay, and no one was *going* to know. At White Lake, I was celibate and lonely. Now, it seemed, my life had taken a turn for the worse. My city persona had been put on hold. Instead, I would be a permanent resident of the small-minded, largely anti-Semitic, decidedly homophobic town of Bethel, New York. My weekend persona would now be my full-time persona. Oy!

The pattern of life I had carved out for myself in upstate New York had been tolerable enough when it lasted for no more than ten weekends in the summer. Over the years, I had even managed to make a few good friends and business acquaintances. My constant need to stir up business for the motel had resulted in my becoming president of the Bethel Chamber of Commerce. Since no one else really wanted the position, I found myself to be the overwhelming favorite. When it came time to vote, I was a shoo-in. Besides, as president, I was in a position to issue all sorts of permits for special events. This gave me a creative outlet as it allowed me to run local arts festivals, plays, concerts, and anything else that might bring people into our town—by way of our motel, of course. This summer was going to be different, though; this summer was going to last three whole months and even beyond, or until my money ran out.

For the Teichbergs, the summer was the busiest time of the year. During the fall and winter seasons, we usually drew only flies. Summer was our so-called "high season"—not that the Teichbergs ever really got high. Over the years, I had noticed that we had three types of customers. First were the old-timers—those few people we had inherited from the former owners of the motel. Most of these folks were well into their seventies and eighties. There was even a ninety-year-old woman named Eva who told stories about how she had made chicken soup for Jean Harlow back in 1932. These relics of earlier times had been coming up to the motel for decades, oblivious to the steady deterioration of their surroundings. Sometimes I thought they kept coming back only because we were the one hotel they knew how to find.

The next category of customers included unsuspecting tourists who discovered too late that all the nice hotels were booked. They were too tired to turn back, and in some cases, they were genuinely lost. Dark, rainy nights helped bring them in, too. There was really no way to predict how many of these tourists would show up during any season, but some of them always did and they were all too easy to spot. They usually arrived just after sundown. First, they would ask for directions; then, for the price of a room. Then, after staying only one night—and sometimes less than an hour— they would come barreling back into the office to demand a refund. In response to any such demands, Momma would shout like a woman with her hair on fire and point maniacally to the sign on the counter that said "Cash only. No refunds." Needless to say, these customers did not return.

The last group of summer customers came courtesy of the Boy Scouts of America. The Ten Mile River Boy Scout Camp was located only a few miles down the road from us. The camp ran three consecutive three-week programs for different groups of kids during the summer. Each group had its own visitors' weekend during which the parents would drive up in their Cadillacs and Lincolns to see how their kids were doing. For the most part, the parents were just as bratty and annoying as the kids, but for those three glorious weekends, at least, the majority of our rooms were booked. The mothers with their beehive hairdos would sit and play canasta, while the fathers downed so many beers at our bar that they actually thought the place wasn't so bad. Why they came to our motel at all always remained a mystery to me. The important thing was that they came.

🌴　🌴　🌴

Getting the motel ready for the summer season took a good deal of work. First, there was the annual paint job. Some time in May, my parents would go to the local Schneerer's Bargain Warehouse to buy cans of cheap white paint. Schneerer's would buy closeout items from manufacturers and stores that had gone out of business, and sell them at lower-than-manufacturer costs. It didn't matter that the paint was already cheap enough; on principle, Momma still had to negotiate the price down. Once we had the cans, Pop would paint the front of only those buildings that could be seen by potential guests pulling into the motel's parking lot. He would often have to paint over the graffiti or swastikas that would appear regularly on our property walls, courtesy of the town's budding Nazi youth.

This year, I decided to repaint the stones I had plucked from our grounds, and arrange them along the grassy paths that led to the various wings of our resort. This created the illusion that there were actual pathways through what was nothing more than fetid swampland. If any cans were left over, Pop would paint as many of the rooms as possible. Since it was hard to decide exactly which rooms were in greatest need of paint, they were refurbished according to room number. If room 9 was the last one painted the year before, we'd begin with room 10 this year. In some cases, it seemed that only the paint kept the bungalows from falling down.

Next, there was the work that needed to be done on the great expanse of lawns and shrubbery. Just like Momma, Mother Nature never made it easy. The lawns all had to be raked of leaves and various other bits of debris. As if that wasn't hard enough, they also had to be mowed. The bushes seemed to grow as quickly as the weeds and would have to be cut back so that our guests could get to their designated rooms without hacking away at the foliage with machetes.

Over the years, the creation of the motel's many signs had been my favorite project. In those first few weeks back at the motel, this job was the only thing that kept me from losing my mind. After I had designed our new "El Monaco" sign, I promptly set about making a second sign from a square section of planking found in Pop's roofing shed. When it was done, I climbed up on Pop's ladder and stoically hammered the square to the gnarled tree trunk behind the main office. The sign simply read, "Help." A day later, I added a few more words. The sign then read, "Help! I'm Nailed to a Tree!"

Whenever I had a free moment, I would run to the barn to make more signs. I decided to let my mind run wild, and the signs became a temporary form of therapy. The coffee shop was now called "Marilyn Monroe's Cup o' Joe Pleasure Mansion," while the small dining area adjacent to the main office was dubbed "Yenta's Pancake House." Of course, all Momma ever made were frozen waffles and her infamous cholent—a stew that I avoided like the plague.

One day, after one of Momma's particularly infuriating rants, I spent the afternoon in the barn creating what may have been that summer's wooden-sign masterpiece. When it had been completed, I hammered it to a tree thirty yards or so from the motel's main office. It read: "Hey, Cossacks—She's Here!"

Aside from my occasional revenge fantasies, these were the usual tasks that occupied the month before we hit our summer stride, which was really nothing more than a slow saunter. That year, however, there was an additional chore: We had to ready our brand-new forty-by-twenty-foot swimming pool for its first season. The pool had been a dream of mine for years. Most of the resorts around us had at least one swimming pool. True, we had White Lake, but so did all the other motels in the vicinity. One of the common questions people always asked was, "Do you have a pool?" Standing behind the counter, completely straight-faced, Momma would reply, "Mister, what you could do here is go jump in the lake." Of course, she didn't even get the joke.

Earlier that year, between my job for the judge and a lawsuit I won against a Park Avenue client, I had saved enough money to finally build my dream pool. By the end of May, the pool had been completed. By the middle of June, Pop had figured out how to fill it with water and work the pump. Because chaise lounges and umbrellas were too expensive, we picked up a dozen or so aluminum beach chairs from Schneerer's. Now we were ready for the season to commence.

🌴 🌴 🌴

The Fourth of July came and went, free of incident but also free of any measurable increase in motel room rentals. Most of the old customers showed up, except for a few who I guessed had moved on to more permanent locations. As I looked at our elderly guests sitting poolside, I was no longer sure that my forty-foot investment would pay off. What I would have given for at least one young handsome hunk diving into that water—but it was not to be with this geriatric set. All I kept thinking was, *If I hadn't spent all my money on this thing, maybe I wouldn't be in this predicament.* At that point, though, I was just trying to keep us from going broke.

As I had done each year since my parents' purchase of the motel, I ran ads in the *Village Voice* looking for aspiring actors who wanted to put on plays in our theater barn in exchange for food and board. As always, we assembled a troupe of ragtag characters and Broadway wannabes—most between jobs waiting on tables—who arrived at White Lake ready to perform. Throughout the summer, we would put on plays, do readings, and hold arts and music festivals on the motel lawns. Unfortunately, except for a handful of guests, my sister Renee, and my milkman, Max, few came to witness our backwoods spectaculars despite my enticing and colorful signs advertising, "To Spritz or not to Spritz . . . Behold the Yiddish *Hamlet.*" Momma went on and on about how we were insane for such foolishness. Of course, her ranting only inspired me to consider staging a production of *The Taming of the Shrew,* with my parents in the starring roles throwing matzoh balls at each other from opposite sides of the barn stage.

Between general maintenance, sign painting, and our summer theater, the Motel of the Damned kept me busy during the day, but the nights were another matter completely. In the first few weeks of June, I went to bed totally exhausted. I'd close my eyes and the very next thing I knew, it was five in the morning. By the middle of July, however, as tired as I often felt, sleep seemed to elude me as my head filled with worries. First, I would feel the nagging fear that I was still on Charley's hit list. Next, I imagined the motel going bankrupt, my family out in the street, and Momma still blaming me for everything. I would finally nod off only to be jolted awake, soaked in sweat and filled with anxiety. Often, in the middle of the night, I would wander off to the coffee shop to make myself an egg cream or two. Sometimes, I would play Judy Garland albums quietly on the record player next to my bed.

The days seemed to pass at a snail's pace. The sleepless nights only intensified my feelings of loneliness and misery. By mid-August, it took an extreme effort to get anything done during the day, and I found myself constantly exhausted. My feelings of sorrow had turned into a deep and unremitting sense of loss and isolation. I went through the motions of my daily activities but didn't really care about anything—not the motel, the recent events in New York City, Charley's possible retribution, or anything else. I had become just like my father—passing through life without actively participating in it. We would walk past each other like a pair of irretrievably lost souls. I'd look at him and see only emptiness in his eyes. I wondered if my eyes had that same detached look. Worse yet, I had stopped caring. If I was turning into my father, so be it.

Finally, Labor Day arrived, marking the end of the summer season. We wouldn't officially close up the motel until mid-winter, but it didn't really matter because no guests checked in during September and my parents would be there year-round anyway. Now, I would be joining them. Closing would mean only draining the pool and taking down a few of the signs. So on Labor Day, at around ten in the morning, I began emptying the water out of the pool. Several of the elderly guests, stationed poolside, began to complain. Mind you, these were people who hadn't set foot in the pool the entire summer. I told them that our lifeguard had just left for the season, and we were required by law to close the pool. That seemed to quiet them down. The fact that we never had a lifeguard didn't seem to occur to them.

By eight that evening, the last of our summer guests had checked out and my day was officially over. I wandered back to the pool to see if the pump was working. It was; the pool was nearly empty. Forty thousand gallons of water had just been emptied into the swampland directly behind us. I sat down on one of the aluminum beach chairs facing the almost-empty pool. However, what I saw was not a pool but just a big hole in the ground—much like my life. The high season was over, and my own low season was now about to begin. Bad enough that I was permanently living upstate, but without the daily tasks needed to run the motel, what in hell was I going to do with myself? Had my life actually sunk to a point where I would miss cutting the weeds and cleaning the toilets?

🌴 🌴 🌴

By mid-September, Bethel looked like a ghost town. Summer was over for most people and the kids were back at school. Of course, life was going on as usual in the big city, but this time, it was going on without me. Occasionally, I would be summoned by Momma to take care of some task on the motel grounds. Like my father, I simply did what was asked without response or complaint.

Earlier in the season, I had pretty much worn out all my brushes while painting my mental-health motel signs. In need of supplies, I figured I would go to the nearby town of Liberty to pick up some sable brushes at the art shop.

Liberty was situated northeast of us, just off Route 17B. It was twice the size of Bethel and had one major advantage—a real downtown business section. Over the years, I had become friends with Ernie Pinkert, the owner of Liberty's art supply store. Ernie was a local legend. If you were an artist and you needed supplies, Ernie either had them in stock or would be able to get them for you within a couple of days. While I picked out some new brushes and a few brightly colored paints, Ernie asked me how things were going.

"Honestly, I don't know," I said. "What I do know is that I'll be staying up at the motel from now on."

Ernie looked at me for a moment or two. He then asked, "Have you ever considered giving art lessons locally? There are lots of folks here who would love to paint if you just got them started."

"I've thought of it once or twice," I replied. "I've just never had a place I could teach without Momma coming in and telling everyone how useless art is."

"Well, you have a place now if you want it," Ernie said, sweeping his arm to indicate his store. "It's not much, but I have an area down in the basement, and I could set up a studio for you to teach art. You don't even have to pay me for the space since I'd be selling paints, brushes, and canvases to everyone who takes the classes. What do you say?"

Without giving it much thought, I heard myself say, "Yes." Ernie was pleased, but by the time I had paid for the brushes and was headed back to the El Monaco, I wasn't so sure. Did I really want to teach finger painting to kindergartners or proper brush-stroke technique to retirees? I knew I needed to get out of the motel once in a while, but was this the best way to do it?

By the following week, Ernie had managed to line up quite a number of students. The classes would be offered on Mondays and Thursdays. While there were no kindergartners to be found, there were several little old ladies who thought that if Grandma Moses could make a lot of money by painting pictures, they could, too. And, of course, a few men showed up, hoping there'd be a nude model or two.

For several weeks, I managed to come in and teach the classes. I don't know the effect the classes had on my students, but they had a profound effect on me because I soon realized how much the simple act of painting truly meant to me. The more I watched the novice painters try to capture the image of a flower arrangement or a view of the Catskill Mountains, the more I understood how I missed that special part of my life—the time I spent designing room layouts, creating color palettes for clients, or simply putting paint to canvas. In the middle of October, I apologized to Ernie and told him that I could no longer teach the classes.

During the years I'd spent in the city, the two things I'd forgotten about upstate New York were how quickly the weather could change, and how spectacular the scenery could be when the leaves were clothed in their autumn colors. While the motel may have been an eyesore, the land all around it became a staged masterpiece of nature. Unfortunately for me, the more I saw of it, the more invisible I felt. I was a lost speck in the universe. I was a motel care-taker who no longer cared.

By mid-autumn, I had developed an evening ritual. After dinner, I would go to the coffee shop, where I'd prepare an egg cream in a tall mug. I would bundle up, go outside, and—with the egg cream in one hand and a beach chair in the other—slowly descend the steps of the empty swimming pool. Finally, I would place the chair in the deep end of the pool and slump my body into it. Slowly sipping my egg cream, I would stare at the white inner walls of the pool until the stars came out. At that point, I would tilt my head back and stare at the celestial bodies above. I would stay like that for hours, sometimes wondering if this was what it was like to be dead. The beach chair was a little uncomfortable, but I supposed that the minor discomforts of a flimsy chair would be less of a problem once I was really dead. At eleven or twelve in the evening, I would make my way back to my assigned room and go to sleep. And I'd really sleep.

As I sat at the bottom of the pool those nights, I could hear sounds of the woodland creatures above me. Birds, crickets, raccoons—I hated the sounds of the woodland creatures. I always made sure to close the gate to the pool behind me and keep those varmints out. One night, I had an idea. I went to my room and brought back a stack of Judy Garland records and the small record player I'd saved from my city apartment. I attached the player to a sixty-foot-long extension cord and plugged it into an outlet in one of the nearest bungalows. I then carried my record player into the empty pool and put on several Judy LPs.

The music played, that beautiful voice rang out, and something inside me began to stir. I found myself thinking back to that crazy night on the *S.S. Peter Stuyvesant* only a few months before. So much had happened to me so quickly after that evening—so much hurt, fear, worry, and loss—that I had forgotten perhaps the most important event of all: I had met and talked to Judy Garland.

I started to replay our short meeting in my mind. Although the time we had spent together was brief, I recalled odd little things that she had mentioned. Had she actually asked me if I was a Catholic? How had she ended up seated behind an upturned banquet table on the main deck of the boat? I closed my eyes and remembered how fragile her arm felt when I cradled it as we spoke. With my eyes closed and her music playing all around me in the empty pool, I felt as if she was once again seated beside me.

As I thought back on my conversation with Judy, I tried to recall something she had said at the end of our talk. What the hell was it? Something about flying witches? No, Momma would never get on a plane—or a broom, for that matter. Something about courage? On that night, courage was something that I certainly did not possess, so it couldn't have been that. And then it came to me. She had talked about what "home" really was. Surprisingly, she hadn't said "There's no place like home"—quite the opposite. According to Judy, home is wherever you hang your hat. Since I had been a devotee of Miss Garland for nearly as many years as I had been alive, there was very little that I didn't know about her. Judy had always been on the move, roaming from one place to another like a gypsy. She never had the chance to settle in one place long enough to establish roots. But what if she didn't *want* roots? Maybe that night on the ship, Judy was trying to tell me that it really didn't matter whether you had roots as long as you were able to do what you loved most in life. If you were following your heart's desire, you were home.

In my escape to Manhattan years before, I had managed to build a lavish home and to surround myself with all sorts of luxuries, but that had never truly fulfilled me. I had become so intensely concentrated on the *things* in my home—my crystal chandeliers, my oriental rugs, my one-of-a-kind dining table—that I had forgotten that life is more than objects. It is about doing what has meaning for you and sharing every day with people you care about and who care about you.

As Judy's spirited version of "Get Happy" echoed against the walls of the swimming pool, I did something that I hadn't done in months: I laughed and laughed and laughed, until tears came to my eyes. These were tears of relief, though, not of sorrow. I rose from the beach chair and danced to Judy's sweet, sweet music—just me alone in the empty pool, with the stars of the dark country night my only audience.

Years before, when I had decided to move out on my own, Renee was the first person I told. Once again, I called Renee and told her I was leaving my parents' home, but this time, she was thrilled. She had been worried about me because she knew that the El Monaco was sucking me dry and that I needed to get my life back. Always caring, Renee said that if I was out of money, I was welcome to stay in her home in New Jersey—just until I could get back on my feet. I thanked her but said that I really had to be in Manhattan. That's where my work and my life were.

Now it was time to tell my parents. I explained that if I didn't get back to the city right away, I would be completely out of money in less than three months. My mother was her usual supportive, encouraging self.

"Mine dummkopf son, he still thinks he's the Mr. Big Shot!" she shouted. "Just go back and see what'll happen to you. They're going to fire you again." Momma delivered pronouncements upon my head just as I had expected. "Nobody fires a rabbi," she added.

A great deal had changed since my early morning return to White Lake several months before. With renewed energy and a relative sense of inner peace, I responded, "You know, some rabbis *do* get fired." That was all I needed to say to set her off. She went on and on, but I didn't care.

Knowing that my parents still required my help, I assured my father that I would spend the workweeks in Manhattan and the weekends at White Lake. This would enable me to earn the money needed to safeguard the motel while still helping with maintenance. Although Momma continued to rant, she knew I'd be back . . . such was the unspoken dance of our dysfunction. The next day in the barn, when Momma wasn't around, my father gave me fifty dollars and wished me luck. I took it again. It had worked the last time.

🌴 🌴 🌴

When I had started out on my own many years before, leaving home was both an escape and an adventure. After all, I was an eighteen-year-old kid who wasn't responsible for anyone but myself. Now it would be different. I was heading back to an uncertain future with a mortgage strapped to my back. But at least I was heading back and I was no longer hiding from the past. How was I going to do it? That was the question. Finding a cheap studio in the Village was not an option. Unsure of how exactly to start, I decided to thumb through my Rolodex, just as I had done in June, when the roof of my life had caved in on top of me.

This time, I searched for and found the Shapiros under the letter "V"—probably for "Very nice people." I hadn't been able to reach them by phone in June, but thought it was time to try again. I felt nervous, but I really wanted to make contact with these people who had once treated me like a member of their family.

I dialed the Shapiros' number and held my breath. Lou and Erica must have picked up different phones in separate areas of their home, because they answered at the same time. Still nervous, I told them who I was.

Once the Shapiros knew it was me, they sounded as delighted to hear my voice as I was to hear theirs. "Elliot, Elliot," Erica said. "How have you been? Where are you? We tried to reach you, but your line had been disconnected. We wondered what had happened to you."

I explained that I had given up my apartment in the city and had moved up to White Lake. "You're in White Lake?" Erica asked.

"Yes, I am," I replied, a big smile on my face as I recalled how much I had always enjoyed talking with them.

"Are your parents okay?" Erica asked.

"Yes," I responded, "they're the same as always, but it was a tough summer up here for them, so I had to stay on full-time."

I wasn't ready to tell them all the humiliating details of my pre-summer fiasco with Charley and the mob. Instead, I explained that I had hit some rough times and had needed the summer to regroup before returning to the city. I told them that I had tried to contact them back in June, and when they didn't answer, I had assumed that they were away on vacation. I then asked why they had tried to reach me.

There was a hushed silence on the other line. Lou started to speak, but his trembling voice trailed off. Erica said simply, "Jon passed away, Elliot. He . . . he died in late June. We just wanted to let you know."

The words hit me like a punch to the gut. I knew how close they had been to their son and couldn't find the words to express how I felt. I said simply, "I won't keep you on the phone. I'm really just so very sorry to hear about Jon."

"No, it's okay, Elliot," Erica said. "Jon always enjoyed your company—he thought you were very funny. I think talking is good. Please, talk with us."

"If I can ask, what happened? Was it an accident?" I asked.

"No. Jon . . . uh, Jon was ill." Lou spoke in a voice that was only a little stronger than before. "He died of complications brought on by pneumonia. It wasn't easy. He had been losing weight for a while. The doctors told us his immune system had practically shut down, and there was very little they could do. They said they'd seen this happen to others but couldn't explain why it was happening. We were all with Jon, though, when it was time for him to come home."

I understood that Lou was referring to heaven when he spoke of his son coming home, and though I couldn't find it in myself to believe in that kind of home, I felt sincere sorrow for their loss. I started to cry. They started to cry. It took some time before any of us could say anything. And then it struck me—how self-absorbed I had been in thinking that I was the only one who had gone through hell over the last few months. My problems paled in comparison to what they must have endured. I told them that I had missed them very much, and asked if I could come to see them in the city.

"Sure you can, Elliot," Erica said right away, and Lou insisted that it would be their pleasure to have me in their home again.

I explained that I was just setting out to find a new apartment in the city, and the Shapiros immediately asked if I'd like to stay with them until I was able to get back on track. "It would be so nice to have you spend some time with us, Elliot," said Lou, and Erica added that she would make me a dinner just like the ones she used to prepare in the old days. She even offered to invite my old friend and mentor Curtis Murray, who had remained in touch with them over the years.

What courageous and lovely people, I thought. More than any other clients, the Shapiros had helped launch my professional life. If nothing else, perhaps I could help them move forward as well. The conversation also reminded me that I had, in fact, once been an independent, successful professional and could be again—in my own way and on my own terms. All I needed was the comfort and support of true friends and another chance at life away from Momma and the El Monaco.

Within a day, I was packed and on the road back to Manhattan. I would stay with the Shapiros, and we would be there for one another as I began my new life in the vibrant atmosphere of the city. Over a period of weeks, with the help of the Shapiros and Curtis, I was able to reconnect with some of my suppliers and a few of my clients. Instead of operating out of my apartment, I used Jon's room. By the end of the month, I had several jobs in hand and was able to bring in some money—enough to keep the El Monaco out of immediate bankruptcy and, eventually, enough to rent a small but decent apartment. So long as it was a place to "hang my hat," my new home would be fine.

So I picked up pretty much where I had left off. As before, I would spend my weekdays in the city as an interior decorator and head back to White Lake on the weekends. This time, though, I was not going to get caught up in a life that didn't bring me any real happiness. Instead, I would try to find a way to be true to myself and remain focused on what brought me joy and satisfaction as an artist, as a gay man, and as a human being. Most of all, I vowed that I would never again allow myself to feel invisible. I now knew that I was the one who had put myself at the bottom of that empty swimming pool.

I had come to realize that I was by no means the only individual whose life was marked by periods of sorrow and despair. Just the same, I felt that it was better to live my life than to lose it. If I hadn't learned that much from my unfortunate run-ins with Charley Gross and Neely Abruzzio, I had certainly discovered it through the graceful example of my friends Lou and Erica Shapiro. Truly wonderful things had already occurred in my life, and I was certain that if I stayed actively engaged in the wide world around me, more extraordinary events lay ahead. Love, friendship, adventure, freedom, joy—it was all there for the taking if I only would allow myself to see it.

If ever I felt unsure or scared, I would listen to my Judy Garland records and recall my delightfully eccentric meeting with her. I would think about the insight that Judy had shared through her few words, and then pull myself out of self-pity and bitterness. I would do this as often as necessary until I found a way back to the home that had been inside me all the while—the home that was me. And whenever I had to draw upon that inner reserve of strength that we all have, I would repeat three words: *Thank you, Judy.*

Epilogue

On June 22, 1969, it was announced that Judy Garland had been found dead from an apparent drug overdose in her London apartment. She had celebrated her forty-seventh birthday just two weeks earlier. The news was a shock. To most Americans, she was the talented performer who had first touched the hearts of millions as she searched for a wizard. To the gay community, she was so much more. Hollywood may have made her a star, but to us, she was an icon. When her funeral was held in New York City, I stood on Madison Avenue, surrounded by tens of thousands of mourners. Strangers tearfully hugged one another as they said good-bye to a lifelong friend.

What Judy Garland represented to the gay community went far beyond her considerable abilities as a singer and actress. Certainly, we loved and admired her work, but more important, we could identify with her as a person. Her life was no bed of roses. She was controlled by the studio that saw her as a commodity rather than a human being. She was in and out of unhappy marriages. She was hopelessly addicted to alcohol and drugs. And with all of that, she still managed to step onto a stage and give her audiences everything she had. Her pain was evident, but so was the joy she found in singing to us—in giving us part of herself.

Like thousands of other gays, I had grown up in a society that had labeled my instinctive behavior both deviant and criminal. While I may have searched for fulfillment in the arms of another man, I did it in spite of how the rest of the world viewed me. I was a second-class citizen. My rights were limited, I knew the dangers, and still, I would not give up. Like Judy Garland's performance, my existence was a constant contradiction. I loved Judy because she expressed both vulnerability and strength in a way that gave me solace.

On the night of June 28, just shy of a week after Judy's death, I was in Manhattan, sharing my grief and my memories of Judy with gay friends at the Stonewall Inn in Greenwich Village. A hot spot for gays, Stonewall was also the target of many police raids at a time when homophobic politics ran rampant. On that summer night, united by our sorrow for the loss of Judy, the gay and lesbian community found the strength to stand up and fight back against police harassment. When the riots had ended, the American gay rights movement was officially born.

What was going to happen next? I wondered. Hell, everyone— gay and straight—was wondering that in 1969. With my beloved Judy now far beyond the rainbow, our country only a few weeks away from putting a man on the moon, and the Vietnam War defining a generation, the answer to my question came in the form of an upstate celebration of music, love, and peace popularly known as Woodstock. But that's another story for another time.

After 1969, answers arrived in many different ways. There was Andre Ernotte, the love of my life. There was my time in Brussels. There was *Rue Haute,* my best-selling novel and first feature film. And in 2007, thanks to a chance encounter in a TV studio green room, there was the gifted director Ang Lee, who decided to transform my personal story into a motion picture. Like my conversation with Judy, my meeting with Lee fulfilled an important dream and proved again that life—while difficult and even cruel—can provide some wonderful surprises. You just have to open your mind and your heart. You just have to find the courage.

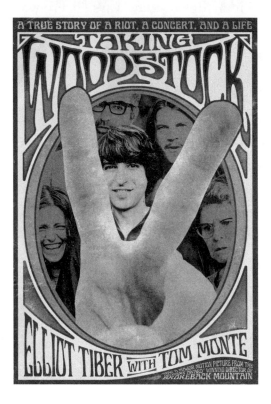